Of Gardens and Graves

Of Gardens and Graves

Kashmir, Poetry, Politics

....

Suvir Kaul

Photographs: Javed Dar

DUKE UNIVERSITY PRESS
Durham and London

Preface © 2017 Duke University Press.
Book originally published as
Of Gardens and Graves: Essays on Kashmir / Poems in Translation,
© Three Essays Collective 2015, India.
All rights reserved
Printed in the United States of America on acid-free paper ∞
Typeset in Garamond Premier Pro by Westchester Publishing Services

Library of Congress Cataloging-in-Publication Data
Names: Kaul, Suvir, author, translator. | Dar, Javed, photographer.
Title: Of gardens and graves : Kashmir, poetry, politics /
Suvir Kaul photographs: Javed Dar.
Description: Durham : Duke University Press, 2016. |
English and Kashmiri (Kashmiri in roman). |
Includes bibliographical references and index.
Identifiers: LCCN 2016030241 (print) | LCCN 2016031241 (ebook)
ISBN 9780822362784 (hardcover : alk. paper)
ISBN 9780822362890 (pbk. : alk. paper)
ISBN 9780822373506 (e-book)
Subjects: LCSH: Kashmir, Vale of (India)—Poetry. | Kashmir,
Vale of (India)—Politics and government—21st century. |
Kashmiri poetry—Translations into English. |
Kashmiri poetry.
Classification: LCC DS485.K27 K38 2016 (print) |
LCC DS485.K27 (ebook) | DDC 954/.6053—dc23
LC record available at https://lccn.loc.gov/2016030241

Cover art: A woman mourns in front of her house, gutted by fire,
Frislan Pahalgam, November 2012. Photo by Javed Dar.

Contents

Illustrations

Preface

From History tears learn a slanted understanding
of the human face torn by blood's bulletin of light.

—AGHA SHAHID ALI, "Of Light"

For the past twenty-five years, unnatural deaths have spoken powerfully of life in Kashmir. One such death occurred on October 29, 2015, when Abu Qasim, the local commander of Lashkar-e-Taiba, an important militant group operating in Kashmir, was killed in an operation conducted jointly by the Indian Army and Jammu and Kashmir Police. Not surprisingly, police spokesmen celebrated the killing of Qasim, the "terrorist," whom they held responsible for several attacks in Kashmir and for ambushing and killing a specialist counterinsurgency police officer, Altaf Ahmad. Soon after Qasim's killing, public protests broke out in parts of Kulgam (where he was killed), and in the adjoining South Kashmir districts of Pulwama and Anantnag, as well as in Srinagar, capital of the state of Jammu and Kashmir. Every time a militant is killed by one of the security forces operating in Kashmir, locals who knew him or knew of him take to the streets to protest and to throw stones at the police. This was not unusual—locals have also been known to throw stones to impede the actions of security forces as they battle militants. At funerals for dead militants, mourners gather in the thousands. They join in anti-India slogans as well as slogans that speak of the martyrdom of the dead man and the certainty that such martyrs will bring *azadi*, freedom, to Kashmir.

The death and funeral of Abu Qasim were no different, even though he was not a local, but, according to the police, a Pakistani from Multan. A vast crowd, more than ten thousand people, assembled for his burial in Bugam village. As on other such occasions, when the crowd dispersed, clashes broke out between some of the mourners and the police and arrests were made. In retaliation against stones thrown at them, members of the security forces damaged cars and smashed the windowpanes of homes in the village (another response that has become routine in Kashmir). What followed however was comparatively unusual, because so beloved was Abu Qasim to people in the area, that after his death different villages competed for the honor of hosting his grave, and once he was buried in Bugam, villagers from Khandaypora attempted to exhume his body for reburial in their village.[1] That is one version of this event. Another tells us that the Khandaypora villagers who attempted the exhumation claimed that Abu Qasim was in fact their relative, a man called Muhammad Yaqoob Hajam who had left the village as a fifteen-year-old to go to Pakistan for weapons training and had since grown, in careful anonymity, into this leader of the Lashkar-e-Taiba.[2] Meanwhile in Srinagar, the Kashmir High Court Bar Association, uncertain about just how to respond to this confusion about Qasim's origins, but certain about the importance of his death, issued a statement applauding his "sacrifices": "All the members were unanimous in saying that as to whether the slain militant was Abdul Rahman of Multan or Mohammad Yaqoob Hajam of Khandaypora Kulgam, he was true, sincere and dedicated soldier of the ongoing freedom struggle and it will take a lot of time to fill the void created by his death."[3]

"Terrorist" or "dedicated soldier of the ongoing freedom struggle": this contrast of language and worldview exemplifies one of the key divides that structure contemporary Kashmir. Terms like these have been used across the world for two centuries now to delegitimize or champion non-state actors who fight in the service of their political ideas against state power. They have a particular salience in our moment, given the rise of Islamophobia and of militants who fight in the name of Islam. It is of course impossible to cordon off discussions about Kashmiri politics from these global debates, especially as they affect the way in which tensions between India and Pakistan are articulated. But even as this book will refer to the imbrication of the global and the local, it will argue that the conflict in Kashmir should be understood on its own terms, that is, by focusing squarely on the specificities of its geographical location and its history. While religious difference is of great and continuing consequence in Kashmir, so too is the state's colonial history. The territories that comprise the state were won in battle by the British and sold in 1846 to the Hindu

Dogra ruler of Jammu, Gulab Singh.[4] The Dogra rulers were particularly exploitative of their impoverished Muslim peasant subjects, whose labor (often unpaid) enabled royal wealth. Muslims were not the only impoverished people in the state, but they were the majority, which meant that their struggles for less exploited lives were put down with the greatest ferocity. The memory of these struggles continues to irrigate Kashmiri Muslim mobilizations against the dominance of non-Kashmiri rulers; these memories are not shared by non-Muslims in the state or indeed by Indians more generally.

It is safe to say that most Indians and some Kashmiris, and certainly the central government in India and the state government in Jammu and Kashmir, hold that a politically misguided and sectarian secessionist movement, aided and armed by Pakistan (this is why Abu Qasim's Pakistani origins are important to them), has torn apart Kashmiri society for the past twenty-five years. Further, it has done incalculable harm to Kashmir's and India's secular identity by causing the fearful exile of the tiny minority of Kashmiri Hindus. In contrast, for many Kashmiris, the majority of them Muslim, their long-term, democratic aspirations for self-determination have been crushed by an illegal occupation, whose edicts are enforced by local collaborators, particularly the politicians elected to state office. For Kashmiri Muslims who believe that their lives should be shared with their coreligionists in the Islamic Republic of Pakistan, the demographic logic that was putatively the basis of drawing borders between the independent nations of India and Pakistan in 1947 should have resulted in large sections, if not all, of the erstwhile princely state of Jammu and Kashmir being incorporated into Pakistan. Others have no wish to be part of Pakistan—for them azadi is just that, political independence. And even those Kashmiri Muslims who are content to remain in India believe that the autonomy of their state, enshrined in Article 370 of the Constitution of India, must be respected at all times. The fact that the state now takes its orders not just from the political and civil machinery in New Delhi, but is de facto under the control of the Indian army and paramilitary forces, not to mention its intelligence agencies, is seen as a massive erosion of the freedoms guaranteed by the Indian government as the price of Jammu and Kashmir's "accession" to India in October 1947. (I discuss this contentious history in later chapters.)

As this book shows, the violence that has come to define Kashmiri lives is not one that features only armed fighters and the soldiers of the various Indian security forces. Ordinary people have paid an extraordinary price too, targeted occasionally by militants either because they serve the state (this was the case with several Pandits murdered in 1989 and 1990, or Muslims killed then and now) or because their loyalties are considered suspect. But by far the largest number of Kashmiri Muslims have been killed, or caused to disappear, by Indian soldiers and paramilitaries who do not trust them and who, more often than not, treat them as the enemy. For every civilian killed or missing, hundreds more have known the fear that attends the intrusive cordon-and-search operations of the security forces ("crackdown" is now part of the vernacular) or the abrasive actions of the police and paramilitaries at manifold checkpoints in cities or villages. The overwhelming sense of a community under siege grows stronger as these experiences are told and retold, and shared anger and mortification work to confirm political antagonism. For a decade and more now, observers of Kashmir have noted the high incidence of cases of post-traumatic stress disorder; the psychic and affective wounds of war are visible everywhere.[5]

....

The essays in this book were written in an effort to come to terms with the state of affairs in Kashmir by reporting both on the embattled condition of Kashmiri lives in recent years and by turning to older histories and political events that have shaped the present. As I explain later, this book was born out of my disquiet with what I, an Indian and a Kashmiri Pandit, saw on the streets of Srinagar and elsewhere in the valley on visits I made to my family home in Srinagar after 2003. The security forces had an intrusive and demanding presence (the level of surveillance waxed and waned over the years, depending on local situations). It was clear that the soldiers did not treat Kashmiris as fellow citizens possessed of civic and political rights. Over the years, even when spokesmen for the Indian Army or the Jammu and Kashmir Police announced that the militancy had been effectively crushed and that only a small number of militants remained, their procedures and actions on the ground continued to be muscular and unyielding. Yes, public protests had led to the removal of some particularly invasive bunkers, but it remained the case that any protest, particularly those that featured young men throwing stones at the paramilitary and police, would frequently end with a protestor or more killed. Further, as civil rights activists began to put together dossiers of information on those civilians who had been killed in "encounters" or had disappeared in these years, as well as on the masses of unmarked graves that were being identified across the valley and in the border areas, it became clear just how much damage had been done in the name of national security. Worst of all, there was and is no redress available to the families of those who have been arrested and caused to disappear or have been killed. The Armed Forces Special Forces Act (AFSPA) protects soldiers from civilian courts, and trials conducted by the army routinely find their own innocent of the crimes of which they are accused. A Public Safety Act (PSA) allows the police and civilian authorities to imprison people without trial, for six months in the first instance but renewable up to two years, and thousands have been subject to such detention.

In order to understand better all that I was seeing in Kashmir, which was so at odds with my experience of life there before 1989, I also began to read about the history of the princely state of Jammu and Kashmir, particularly during the vexed period of the Partition of British India into the independent nations of Pakistan and India. As a state ruled by an Indian king with treaty relations with the British, Jammu and Kashmir was outside of the purview of the Boundary Commission headed by Sir Cyril Radcliffe, which meant that its Hindu ruler, Hari Singh, would determine the fate of his majority Muslim subjects by deciding whether to join India or Pakistan. Hari Singh seems to have harbored hopes of maintaining an independent kingdom, but his legitimacy had been weakened by domestic protests against his autocratic rule, and when a column of irregulars from Pakistan entered Kashmir and neared Srinagar, Hari Singh signed an instrument of accession to India (in which he gave up authority over defense, foreign affairs, and communications) and fled south. Indian forces flew into Srinagar and fought off the invasion, a battle that led to the first extended border warfare between India and Pakistan. When a United Nations mediated ceasefire was declared on January 1, 1949, the "lines of control" established during the battles between the Indian and Pakistani armies froze into borders. As a consequence, depending on their location, subjects of the erstwhile state were now—de facto—citizens of one nation or the other.

Indian Kashmir (which is the area of the state that is the subject of this book) owes its present territory to this military history, but that does not in itself provide an explanation of the present-day state of affairs there. While I do call attention to some important events in the years after 1949, this book is not an exercise in political history as much as it is an effort to call attention to the political and civic life of Kashmiris after 1989, which is when an armed secessionist movement transformed life irrevocably. The response of the Indian government, particularly when it became clear that these fighters were being trained in and supported by Pakistan, was predictably vigorous, and Kashmir was transformed into an extended encampment for government forces. The security footprint is now huge and unlikely to shrink any time soon. No matter what other, more pacific, attempts either the state or the Indian government make to weld Kashmir to India, it is clear to them that without the use of force, or the ever-present threat of force, Kashmir will spiral out of their control. Thus, these administrators seem to have decided that some degree of violence is necessary to govern Kashmir, which is why they are unlikely to suspend either the AFSPA or PSA or ask the army or paramilitaries to return to their cantonments in the border districts alone. If there is any one lesson that I have learned in writing this book, it is that Kashmir has been effectively militarized, and that we will live with the consequences of that militarization for a long time to come.[6]

In Kashmir today, and by extension, in discussions of Kashmir elsewhere, there is little agreement about such histories of territory and state formation, of cultural and social organization, of religious and confessional practices, and of intercommunity relations. This is scarcely surprising, for there is no discussion of the political present and future in Kashmir that does not offer its own version of the past. Further, the great alienation of Kashmiri Muslims and Pandits (which is what Kashmiri Hindus are called) from each other means that they have generated increasingly partisan accounts of their past and that of their homeland, *Kasheer*, in order to ratify the political divides of the present.[7] This historiographical divide, if it can be called that, is mirrored in all modes of public conversation: newspapers in Kashmir report events routinely ignored by Indian newspapers, particularly the myriad conflicts between Kashmiris and the security forces, and their editorials take positions that are anathema to the nationalist press in India. Further, these ideological divisions also play out between the Muslim-majority province of Kashmir and the Hindu-majority province of Jammu, and to some extent across the Muslim-majority districts and the Buddhist-majority areas of Ladakh (the third province of the state of Jammu and Kashmir).

These polarizations have eroded the memory of shared lives, lives lived across confessional differences but fully aware of common reservoirs of cultural memory. Kashmiris—Pandit or Muslim—shared a language, *Koshur* (more widely known as Kashmiri), which differentiated them from Hindus and Muslims elsewhere in the state or indeed in India or in Pakistan. Kashmiri, spoken and written with provincial accents and variations, drew upon both Persian and Sanskrit vocabularies and literary traditions, and its folklore was shared across religious and ethnic divides. Today, even the term used for this supposedly composite culture, *Kashmiriyat*, is discredited as a retrospective illusion disseminated by a state machinery whose task was to cement Muslim Kashmir to Hindu India. Pandits and Muslims, some now argue, shared little: Pandit ideologues claim that they always lived in fear of the majority who forced them into exile from their homes at several points in the past; their Muslim equivalents remember only that Pandits were the henchmen of the aggressively exploitative rule of a Hindu (though non-Kashmiri) ruler. Within Kashmir today, occasional efforts are made to build bridges between Muslims and Pandits, but few have had any success. Polarization, rather than reconciliation, remains the order of the day. The generations who shared lives are aging and dying, and now young Pandits who have grown up outside Kashmir in conditions of forced exile or young Muslims who grow up in Kashmir experiencing the punitive might of the state apparatus find little reason to empathize with one another. In recent years, Pandits have returned to visit Kashmir, particularly the shrines and temples where they once congregated, but many avoid the city neighborhoods or villages they called home. And in spite of sporadic efforts made by the government to enable them to come home, hardly any one has returned.[8]

....

The essays will show that even as much changes in Kashmir—elections are held, competing political parties replace each other in government, the Indian government announces different initiatives designed to address Kashmiri demands—much, particularly the alienation of the majority

Muslim population, remains the same. If anything, the passage of time has deepened their alienation and conviction that no political or any other kind of justice is available from Indian rulers, their security services, and indeed the Kashmiri political parties that are elected to office in the state or in the Parliament of India. Today as I write, the state government has blocked the Internet, arrested hundreds of people, including the entire leadership of those political parties that stand for independence, and has imposed a massive security operation to allow the Indian prime minister to fly into Srinagar to hold a public rally (an oppositional political rally has been denied permission).[9] In the past, the government machinery has coerced people into attending official rallies; this occasion is no different.

There is a major difference though, between this state government and those in the past. In December 2014, state elections were held in Jammu and Kashmir, and the People's Democratic Party (PDP) won the highest number of seats, followed by the Hindu-identified Bharatiya Janata Party (BJP), and a coalition government between these parties replaced the National Conference-Indian National Congress coalition that had formed the previous government. The PDP had fought the elections by reiterating its commitment to the constitutional provisions that guarantee Jammu and Kashmir a degree of autonomy within India, a commitment that clashed with the stated objective of the BJP to incorporate the state even more firmly into the Union of India. However, the PDP and the BJP managed to work out a common minimum program, and the government was sworn in on March 1, 2015. Some observers saw in this unlikely alliance the chance for innovative solutions to the political problem of Kashmir; they argued that only a Hindu-identified, hard-line "nationalist" government in Delhi, such as that of the BJP and its allies, would be able to risk political capital enough to launch negotiations with the "separatist" politicians of Kashmir and possibly even with Pakistan. These hopes have since been belied. The electoral dominance of the BJP, far from resulting in any form of innovative governance or strategic planning in India, has entrenched their right-wing, Hindu-centric politics, with the result that Indian minorities, particularly Muslims, are even more fearful for their rights. This polarization has, not surprisingly, ossified existent political divides between a Hindu-majority Jammu and a Muslim-majority Kashmir too.

Indian politicians and policy planners as well as their allies in Kashmir insist that the problem of Kashmir is in essence a problem of regional underdevelopment, to be ameliorated by offering large financial "development packages" to the state. On this visit, the Indian prime minister has announced a grant of $12 billion. However, in the protests that accompanied his visit, a college student, Gowhar Ahmad Dar, was killed when the paramilitary fired at protestors, his death a reminder to Kashmiris of the besieged state of their lives.[10] The new funds offered by the prime minister—if and when they materialize into projects that improve public services—will not cause too many Kashmiris to change their political aspirations, or indeed their sense that such central assistance comes at the price of a refusal to address their political demands. Quite simply, "Indian" violence has damaged "Kashmiri" lives for too long now for the latter to think of India as a nation committed to development; for them, India is a state that holds their lives hostage to its international and provincial security strategies. Ironically, more money in the system tends only to enhance one of the key paradoxes of Kashmiri life: even as the social compact between India and the state, between the administration and citizens, between Jammu and Kashmir, between Kashmiri Muslims and Pandits, is broken, houses in Kashmiri cities and towns, and now in villages, grow larger and more opulent, as do the shopping malls and stores. Not all Kashmiris share in these spoils, of course, but it is impossible not to notice the contrast between the everyday civic and political vulnerability of ordinary people and the steadily growing wealth and power of the elites who rule them.

....

This book is far from the first to call attention to the political, cultural, and existential dimensions of the conflict in Kashmir. I have drawn upon the work of historians, journalists, activists, political scientists and others, as I have the less systematic but no less powerful social media postings of scores of Kashmiris who have learned to archive in the moment their experiences, their anger, their insights, and their frustrations. The work of documentary and feature filmmakers, artists, novelists, and poets has borne urgent witness to these times, and I turn to them for inspiration and understanding more than once. Over the last decade and more, it has become clear to observers that no volume of documentation of the suffering of Kashmiris is going to have any substantial impact on policy planners, and that Kashmir is effectively at the mercy of competing Indian and Pakistani nationalisms, a pawn in their larger geopolitical calculations. This is a recognition more debilitating for a scholar like me than it is for Kashmiris who continue to struggle for their political rights, and it is perhaps this impasse that led me to the project that is a substantial part of this book. I began collecting poems written in Kashmiri by both Muslim and Pandit poets in the conflict years, hoping to find in them a durable record of the intensities of feeling that I experienced each time I spoke to Kashmiris about their lives in these years. In Srinagar or elsewhere, conversations have a habit of trailing off, or rather, ending in quotations of phrases and lines from poems in Kashmiri or Urdu; when description and analysis fail, or founder in the same ruts, it is as if meaning can be conveyed only the allusive, condensed power of the poetic fragment.

Kashmiri is a remarkably idiomatic language, and even the more formal, seemingly "elevated" practices of poetry are enriched by the turns of phase, evocative images, and startling metaphors of everyday speech. However much poetic voice is the product of studied artifice, it seems not to stray too far from the language of the community. This is what makes it possible to *read* (and this too is a discipline that has to be learned) in the conventions of poetic compression and repetition, in the cadences of phrases and lines, the trauma, vexations, and conflicted political life of a besieged community. And I use the term "community" in the singular, to include both Muslims and Pandits, no matter that Pandit poets and Muslim poets write of divergent experiences, and seemingly at cross purposes. On occasion they do address each other, but even when they do not, theirs is inevitably the dialogic exchange that results from immersion in a common language and literary history. This is the argument that drives the translations and my readings of poems in this book, and mine is, I believe, an intellectual and critical position demanded by our times. I hope readers will recognize that this method of collecting, translating, and reading poems is as much a performance of the politics and desires of this book as are its critiques of the nation-state that are developed in its more prosaic sections.

A word on the photographs: Javed Dar is a news photographer in Srinagar who has over the last decade compiled an astonishing record of life in a conflict zone. His pictures—printed here in black and white—tell powerful stories of people in motion, mobilized in the service of their political aspirations; or moving more quietly, yet always aware of the surveillance that is now routine; or tranquil in moments of contemplation. He records conflict: the police or soldiers in action, or the eerie silences of public spaces cordoned off from civilians and populated only by uniformed men, or civilians and soldiers locked into confrontation. Dar's pictures follow the rhythms of life in Kashmir, with one important proviso: news photographers turn into the eyes, and on video, also the ears, of the community, for they go to places where no others are permitted, and they enable us to see much that official media ignores. In my visits to Srinagar, Dar's pictures served a similarly enabling purpose for me, for there were many days of curfew and street violence where I stayed home but was able to look closely at, and to learn from, the pictures he had taken. I had hoped to use one of Javed's pictures on the cover of this book, but Asad Zaidi and Tarun Bharatiya, the publishers of this book in India were so moved by his portfolio that they decided that these pictures would be a remarkable counterpoint to the poems in this book as well as to the essays. They were right, and I am grateful for their decision and for the insights made available by Dar's photographs.

NOTES

Epigraph from Agha Shahid Ali, "Of Light," in *Call Me Ishmael Tonight*, reprinted in Ali, *The Veiled Suite: The Collected Poems* (New Delhi: Penguin, 2009), 363.

1. "Where Should Abu Qasim Lie Buried? Villagers Clash in Kashmir," *Hindustan Times*, October 31, 2015. Accessed October 31, 2015. http://www.hindustantimes.com /punjab/where-should-abu-qasim-lie-buried-villagers-clash-in-kashmir/story -67W9TbiFYmHKoGYSCEyw8N.html.

2. "Khandaypora Family Still Claims Slain LeT Commander." *Kashmir Reader*, October 31, 2015. Accessed on October 31, 2015. http://www.kashmirreader.com/News /SingleNews?NewsID=336&callto=Top.

3. "Rahman of Multan or Hajam of Kulgam, Qasim Was 'True Soldier of Freedom Struggle': Bar." *Kashmir Reader*, October 31, 2015. Accessed on October 31, 2015. http://www.kashmirreader.com/News/SingleNews?NewsID=828&callto=Area.

4. The Dogra are Rajputs who migrated from Rajasthan and adjoining areas to the plains and hill tracts around Jammu. Dogras, particularly in India, are largely Hindu (most Muslim Dogras or Rajputs live in Pakistan or Azad Kashmir). They speak Dogri, a language that has more in common with Punjabi than with Kashmiri. The British considered them one of the "martial races" of India and recruited them in large numbers into the British Indian Army.

5. There is now a great variety of writing on Kashmir; two very different forms of writing provide a good introduction to the existential circumstances and political history of contemporary Kashmir: Malik Sajad's *Munnu: A Boy From Kashmir* and a special issue

of the journal *Race and Class, Memory and Hope: New Perspectives on the Kashmir Conflict*, ed. Shubh Mathur.

6. The International Peoples' Tribunal on Human Rights and Justice in Indian-Administered Kashmir (IPTK) and the Association of Parents of Disappeared Persons (APDP), two activist Kashmiri human rights groups, have recently released a detailed report on the military footprint in Kashmir and the circles of violence that eddy out of their encampments. *Structures of Violence: The Indian State In Jammu and Kashmir* (Srinagar: Jammu and Kashmir Coalition of Civil Societies, September 2015) is a powerful demonstration and indictment of the varieties of violence that are precipitated in a conflict zone when militaries are allowed to take over land and operate with impunity among civilian populations. Accessed on November 15, 2015. http://www.jkccs .net/structures-of-violence-the-indian-state-in-jammu-and-kashmir-2/. Another recent study also comments pointedly on the army's "land grabs" in Kashmir: Peer Ghulam Nabi and Jingzhong Ye, "Of Militarization, Counter-insurgency and Land Grabs in Kashmir," *Economic and Political Weekly* 46–47, November 21, 2015: 58–64.

7. Chitralekha Zutshi's *Kashmir's Contested Pasts: Narratives, Sacred Geographies, and the Historical Imagination* (Delhi: Oxford University Press, 2014), is a sustained and convincing investigation into traditions of historiography and popular belief in Kashmir. The power of Zutshi's analysis comes in part from her recognition of the effect the great polarizations of the present have had in generating discordant accounts of Kashmiri history.

8. Amit Anand Choudhary, "Only 1 Pandit Family Returned to Valley in 25 Years." *Times of India*, Nov. 1, 2015. Accessed on November 2, 2015. http://timesofindia .indiatimes.com/india/Only-1-Pandit-family-returned-to-Valley-in-25-years/articleshow /49613620.cms.

9. Mudasir Ahmad, "Massive Crackdown in Kashmir to Guarantee 'Peaceful' Modi Visit." *The Wire*, November 6, 2015. Accessed on November 6, 2015. http://thewire.in /2015/11/06/massive-crackdown-in-kashmir-to-guarantee-peaceful-modi-visit-14890/.

10. Aijaz Hussain, "1 Dead in Kashmir Protest as India's Leader Promises Aid." *AP News*. November 7, 2015. Accessed on November 7, 2015. http://bigstory.ap.org/article/a 579f72b11f34bdc9773cf4b41923ec9/indian-kashmir-high-alert-prime-minister-modis -visit.

Acknowledgments

So many to thank, for their advice, encouragement, and expertise. First, Aijaz Hussain and Parvaiz Bukhari, invaluable friends and guides.

For conversations—occasional or more sustained, in person and in print—that extend back a decade and have left indelible marks on this volume: Gowhar Fazili, Muzamil Jaleel, Basharat Peer, Arif Ayaz Parrey, Mohamad Junaid, Fayaz Ahmed Dar, Nawaz Gul Qanungo, Saiba Varma, Mona Bhan, Cabeiri Robinson, Simona Sawhney, Idrees Kanth, Shalini Advani, Neeladri Bhattacharya, Rohit Chopra, Brijraj Singh, Sundeep Dougal, Antoinette Burton, Arjun Appadurai, Mukul Kesavan, and Lauren Goodlad. My colleagues Max Cavitch and David Eng enabled the third chapter, as did Shalini Advani, Michael Rothberg, Saiba Varma and Mona Bhan. Meghna Chandra, and later, Kaushik Ramu, helped clean it all up.

The Race and Empire Discussion Group and the Latitudes Reading Group at the University of Pennsylvania commented on versions of these chapters. Talks based on these essays were given at conferences organized by the Carr Center for Human Rights Policy, Harvard Kennedy School (thanks to Mallika Kaur); the Grounding Kashmir symposium at Stanford University (thanks to Nosheen Ali and Thomas Blom Hansen); the Center for Modern Indian Studies, Georg-August Universität, Göttingen (thanks to Rupa Viswanath); The New School, New York (thanks to Arien Mack and Arjun Appadurai); Bard College at Simon's Rock (thanks to Asma Abbas, David L. Gonzalez Rice and Auritro Majumder); the Unit for Criticism and Interpretive Theory, University of Illinois, Urbana-Champaign (thanks to Lauren Goodlad); and the Society for the Humanities at Cornell University (thanks to Tim Murray). This book was completed while on a Dean's Leave from the School of Arts and Sciences—I am grateful for that, and for the research support enabled by the endowment for the A. M. Rosenthal Professorship at the University of Pennsylvania.

As always, Tariq Thachil and Piyali Bhattacharya. Primla Loomba. Urvi Puri. Kaushalya Kaul.

Sanjay Kak, for inspiration and so much else beyond this volume.

Ania Loomba, who walked curfewed streets with me, insisted that this was a volume worth producing, and then restructured it for me.

Finally, this volume is for my parents, Kaushalya Kaul and the late Bhavanesh Kaul, who persevered in their belief that Srinagar was home, and to Bullee Behan, who makes that possible.

PERMISSIONS

Sections of chapter 1 were first published in *The Telegraph* (Calcutta) on September 1, 2003 ("Srinagar, Four Years Later") and in *Outlook* on September 3, 2008 ("Kashmir's Sea of Stories") and August 6, 2010 ("Days in Srinagar"). The last chapter was republished as "Diary of a Summer" in *Until My Freedom Has Come: The New Intifada in Kashmir*, ed. Sanjay Kak (New Delhi: Penguin, 2011, 17–30; Chicago: Haymarket Books, 2013) and elements of the first two chapters were part of "Two Lives, One Home," in a special issue edited by Ira Pande of the *India International Center Quarterly* 37: 3&4 (2011), 186–197, and reprinted by Pande in her *A Tangled Web: Jammu and Kashmir* (New Delhi: HarperCollins India, 2011).

A version of chapter 2 was published as "An' You will Fight, Till the Death of It. . . .' Past and Present in the Challenge of Kashmir," in *Social Research* 78:1 (2011), 173–202 and reprinted in *India's World: The Politics of Creativity In a Globalized Society*, eds. Arjun Appadurai and Arien Mack (New Delhi: Rupa Books, 2012), 161–189.

Sections of chapter 3 and the coda were first published as "A Time without Soldiers: Writing about Kashmir Today," in *Historical Reflections/Réflexions Historiques* 38:2 (2012), 71–82.

A version of chapter 4 was first published as "Indian Empire (and the Case of Kashmir)," in *Economic and Political Weekly* 47:13 (March 26–April 1, 2011), 66–75.

The author has obtained permissions to reprint and translate poems by all but two of the poets in this volume. The author has not been successful in his efforts to reach them, and we welcome correspondence about this matter from either the poets or their representatives.

Aerial view | Srinagar, August 2011

A house is blown up by government soldiers during a gun battle with militants | Batpora Kulgam, January 2008

Introduction

This volume is based upon essays written over the last decade in an effort to come to terms with what I have seen and felt during yearly visits to Kashmir. In 2003, after a gap of eight years, my parents resumed living in our family home in Srinagar. My father's professional life as a metallurgist had taken him to Bengal and Bihar, but once he retired in 1980, my parents moved to the home my grandfather built in the 1920s. Like some others who thought of Kashmir as home, they were able to afford a flat in Delhi, where they planned to spend the winter months. They followed that pattern for a few years; in 1989, as in earlier years, they moved to Delhi in November. But that winter Srinagar, and Kashmir more generally, altered unimaginably, and though my father made short trips in the next three years to see how our home fared, the grim situation in the city and the breakdown of civil life meant that they were now forced to live in Delhi throughout the year.

They were of course fortunate: most other Pandits, the Kashmiri Hindus who left Kashmir in 1990 and in subsequent years did not have alternate homes. They were cast adrift, as were the Kashmiri Muslim families who also moved because they feared life in the valley or the higher towns and villages. The Pandits suffered in refugee camps in Jammu and other cities in India; they, and those who had access to other accommodation, began to rebuild life outside Kashmir. Initially few thought that their displacement would last long. They expected that once matters stabilized in Kashmir they would return to their own homes, neighborhoods and communities and resume their occupations. But as the months, and then years, dragged on, it became clear that the war-like situation that existed in the valley and in the other districts of Kashmir was not conducive to going home. The decade of the 1990s was marked by constant firefights between the security forces and armed militants fighting for independence, and as the security presence became pervasive and intrusive, civilian lives were inevitably drawn into and disfigured by violence.

Kashmiris suffered outside Kashmir, as they did within: not identically, and not at all for the same reasons. These years drove a huge rift between Muslims, the overwhelming majority in Kashmir, and the Pandits. Whether or not particular Muslim communities or individuals supported the struggle for independence—and there were many who did not—they were at the receiving end of muscular, even brutal methods of policing. As the word "crackdown" became part of the Kashmiri vernacular, Muslim alienation from India increased. The more it became clear that the *tehreek* (movement) was not a simple matter of Pakistan-sponsored *jihadis*, the less Pandits could imagine a place for themselves in Kashmir. Their politics hardened too, and some among them demanded a new homeland carved out of parts of the state of Jammu and Kashmir, one that would be a Hindu-majority province. Another decade rolled painfully by: the largest majority of Kashmiri Pandits rebuilt their lives elsewhere, their language and cultural norms now deterritorialized and in danger of dissolution. In Kashmir, the power of the military, paramilitary, and police decimated the armed *tehreekis* till only a few hundred remained; in the process thousands of Kashmiris disappeared and many were arrested and held without charge. When they were released, they brought news of torture and the maiming of those incarcerated. Few Kashmiris had any trouble believing these stories. In village upon village, in city neighborhoods, civilians were routinely treated by security forces not as Indian citizens with rights but as the enemy, or at least as aiding and abetting the enemy.

This is not a world that—quite literally—could be imagined in the years when I was growing up. I lived in Bengal but with a strong sense that home was in Kashmir, where both sets of my grandparents lived, and where we spent extended summers each year. Ours was a largely Pandit neighborhood, but my grandparents and other relatives had, not surprisingly, many Muslim friends and colleagues, and they came and went from our home. When the first Muslim family moved into a neighboring house, my grandfather welcomed the family, and said that he was glad good people had come to live two houses away. (I have often felt that it was a blessing that both my grandfathers, and one of my grandmothers, passed away before 1990—they had lived within a composite society, and would not have been able to comprehend the speed and the ugliness with which their world was ripped apart.) Our aunts and cousins who lived in Srinagar had studied and taught with their Muslim colleagues; for them, confessional differences mattered little or nothing, and that is the world I visited and enjoyed. Were there tensions? I am sure there were, and now my reading has taught me about signal instances of riots and occasional violence going back to 1931, but in the years when I was growing up there was no polarization or systemic separation in everyday life. On the contrary, Kashmir seemed largely free of the communal riots that periodically scarred other parts of India.[1]

The essays that have been rewritten into chapters in this volume were written at periodic intervals in response to all that I saw and heard in Kashmir, particularly in Srinagar. Being there—simultaneously an outsider and an insider—was deeply disturbing, for the signs of people's suffering were obvious. I was struck by the tone in which so many people described their experiences: even as they talked of enormities of one kind or the other— deaths, beatings, extortion, more everyday forms of humiliation—they did so in matter-of-fact terms. Some had stories of renegade militants to tell, and the ugly demands that they made on the civilian population; most spoke of their treatment at the hands of the men in Indian uniforms. Few would reveal their political beliefs, at least not till they learnt to trust you, and trust was hard to come by in Kashmir. There had been too many betrayals, often by those in positions of power, but also within communities and neighborhoods. In any case life was a strange, even schizophrenic, mix of political and civil administration and the ever-present security forces, and people had learned to fear the actions of both. But fear did not mean that they conformed; on the contrary, they remained quick to come out on to the streets, to challenge the government in speech and act, to mourn and celebrate their dead, including those who died fighting the police and the military.

Over these years, putatively democratic elections have been held and elected governments put in place, but their legitimacy and authority is limited by the power of other political groupings (such as the All Parties Hurriyat Conference[2]) and the myriad Indian security forces. At the same time, the gaps between democratic governance and everyday life, and the constant, wearying friction between the security-state and the civilian population, have become increasingly visible to even casual observers. This is the case even when things are much calmer, with substantial increases in tourist traffic, including the religious tourists who throng to the Amarnath Yatra. Such outsiders flood through, have a very good time, interact productively with Kashmiris, and go their way, remarking on the "normalcy" in Kashmir, but resentment against and resistance to India and Indian power constantly simmer and occasionally explode. This is the situation today too, and it is unlikely that much will change in the near future.[3]

Given the paucity of detailed and analytical national coverage of life in Kashmir in the 1990s, it is possible to understand why people outside Kashmir had not quite grasped all that had happened there—which is a complaint made both by Kashmiri Pandits and Kashmiri Muslims. In the 2000s, however, it became impossible to ignore events in Kashmir—you had to look away not to notice. The mushrooming of the internet meant that hundreds of video clips, taken by amateurs, documented events ranging from firefights between militants and paramilitaries, to political protests, including battles between stone-throwing young men and the police, to funeral processions in which the wails of sorrow and anger were interspersed with slogans demanding azadi (freedom). Reports from Kashmiri and international human rights groups documented the routine suspension of civil rights in this heavily militarized zone, as did Sanjay Kak's *Jashn-e-Azadi* (2007). A new generation of Kashmiris—those who had grown up in the "conflict years"—now called attention to their lives, and their testimonials, their reportage, and their creative work made clear just how much loss and sorrow had defined their lives, whether in Kashmir or outside, in Kashmiri villages or in camps in Jammu. The Indian central government produced its own documents as official "interlocutors" and unofficial mediators wandered in and out, but their recommendations too were quietly ignored.

I began writing on Kashmir, as I said before, to try and understand why Kashmir had erupted with the ferocity that it did, and why it has turned into an intractable problem for Indian democracy. This meant reading about the history of Jammu and Kashmir, for like most Indians (or indeed Kashmiris) of my generation, little of that complicated history, particularly of the Maharaja's accession to India, had been any more than a set of fuzzy tales for me, and until 1990 there had been no real reason to revisit them. In these years, of course, academics and journalists have written on Kashmir, most often in the language of international relations, political science, or public policy (some of the more compelling volumes and essays are footnoted in the chapters that follow). Convincing as such analyses and prognoses might be, they often have too little sense of the texture of people's lives and experiences, which are surely central to their political feelings and aspirations. These chapters, on the other hand, have been motivated by what I experienced and by the conversations I had with people in and outside Kashmir. Of course, even as I reacted to events on the ground I also felt impelled to understand them within a longer historical framework. In particular, I came to believe that the historical analysis of the making of modern nation-states in the moment of European colonialism might offer crucial insights into the formation and practices of a postcolonial nation-state like India (see the last chapter, "Indian Empire [and the case of Kashmir]").

In other chapters I explore elements in the history of Jammu and Kashmir that I came to think had particular bearing on the contemporary conflict. In each case my reading in the past was motivated by events in the present, and often by the despairing sense that not much was getting better in Kashmir. Yes, tourism was up and militancy was down, but there seemed to be no shifting in the political imagination of the Indian state, Indian political parties, or indeed institutions and politicians in Jammu and Kashmir. Years passed, one form of violence was repressed only for another to take its place, interludes of peace were punctured by periods of intense civic unrest—the more things changed the more they seemed the same. How then to represent more fully, with its felt intensities, the political feelings that flooded through Kashmiri lives and conversations?

My enquiries into life in Kashmir also drew upon the questions I explore in my professional life as a teacher and critic of literature, particularly of poetry. In every context I know, and certainly in contemporary Kashmir, poetry offers a rich archive of heightened feelings and desires. Simply put, poems have something important to tell us about lives lived in the face of extraordinary political disruptions and violence. Political debates, policy prescriptions, and historical analyses are of course crucial to understanding a situation as vexed and complicated as that which exists in Kashmir, but there has to be space, and analytical utility, for the evidence contained in cultural production. Here is an example: one of the first poems I read, "Corpse" by Shabir "Azar," struck me as a remarkable instance of the power with which a poem can perform disordered subjectivity, but more particularly, subjectivity cleaved and reconsolidated by recurrent violence. I quote it here:

In the mirror of that lake,
what should I see . . . ?

from its depths
that stranger-like corpse
stares

I have often
thrown a stone—
I wished to smash that mirror

ripples formed, spread, dissipated

and

at the furthest reaches of the silent lake
the same corpse kept staring

the corpse!

as if it would steal
my musings today . . . !
or
fold the imprint of my future
into the vastness of the lake!

Why should I pick up a stone
and smash this mirror

if the corpse
is in the lake

the lake too
is in the corpse

or
both are locked in drops of
water...!⁴

This is a quiet poem, calm and meditative ("reflective," to use the idiom
of the poem), which makes its internal movement even more compelling
and powerful. From the opening of the poem, in which the poet-figure
seeks to commune with nature (such moments are a recurrent feature of
Kashmiri landscape poetry) but finds in the lake not placid beauty but the
floating corpse, to its conclusion, which makes clear that nature (the lake)
is itself now transfigured by death, this poem by Shabir "Azar" is an exercise
in rewriting poetic expectations. It makes clear that one of the primal characteristics of Kashmir's natural beauty, its lakes, which have long been
seen as spaces of rejuvenation, as mirrors in which the thoughtful self can
find spiritual and aesthetic renewal, now provide perverse lessons in the
power of violent, anonymous death to reconfigure the relation between
the self and nature, and thus, the nature of selfhood itself.

Here, the mirror-surface of the lake reflects not the poet's face or indeed the natural features that surround the lake but reveal, surfacing from
its depths, a "stranger-like corpse" that stares back at the poet. Whose is
the corpse? Not that of a stranger, which word would suggest the poet's
certainty that he does not know the dead person. The corpse is "stranger-
like," which emphasizes the poet's uneasiness about whether or not this
corpse is identified or even identifiable, and allows for the fear that the
corpse might, after all, not be that of a stranger. Unknown and yet perhaps
familiar? Anonymous, but perhaps not quite so? This combination of un-
knowing and potential recognition is unnerving, and the next three lines
delineate the poet's discomfort: "I have often/thrown a stone—/I wished
to smash that mirror." The mirror-lake reflects not the poet's pensive isolation but reveals his uncanny double, the corpse. The corpse's presence is
insistent, implacable, and the poet seeks to disrupt it—he throws a stone
to break the lake's surface, but as its ripples swell and dissipate, the corpse
stares still, even at those edges where the ripples die into silence. No
gesture of disavowal, however violent, will prevent the corpse from staring

back at the poet, for the corpse is the only image that appears in this watery mirror.

In this unfortunate mirroring, poetic subjectivity is reconfigured. For the corpse is not an inert presence, but possesses a violent agency that violates the poet's hoped for communion with nature:

the corpse!

as if it would steal
my musings today . . . !
or
fold the imprint of my future
into the vastness of the lake!

The corpse is a threat and a challenge to the poet. It allows no peaceful resolution, no immersion in nature that is not also an immersion into the political implications of such a sight. The corpse has the power to steal the poet's present, to direct his thoughts, but also, even more forcefully, to imprison the poet's future into a common watery vastness. This is the moment of recognition then, the turn in the poem where the poet recognizes that his future might well be no different from the corpse's present, and that the Kashmiri lake in which the corpse now floats may well contain his end too. In this uncanny, unwelcome communion between poet and "stranger-like" corpse lies community.

This forced recognition changes the poet's awareness. He repudiates his past desire to break free of the mirror in whose surface he finds only death and disquiet. The question he now asks, "why should I pick up a stone/ and smash this mirror," is a prelude to a statement that understands that Kashmir, its lakes, its beauty, its people, have been reconfigured by violence. No one stands apart:

if the corpse
is in the lake
the lake too
is in the corpse

or
both are locked in drops of water . . . !

In this dispensation, the corpse and the lake, that is, unnatural death and natural beauty in Kashmir, inform each other. For a poet, the contemplation of nature that once yielded pastoral poetry and perhaps philosophical reflection now forces this political insight. There is recognition, and sad acceptance, for this is the lesson contained and reiterated even in the finished perfection of drops of water.

The witness offered by a poem like this is also the reason I began collecting poems written in Kashmiri during these years of conflict, a selection of which I, working in close collaboration with others, have translated here. I hope they will allow the reader to see that the power of a poet speaking to and for Kashmiris interrogates not only official accounts of Kashmir and Kashmiris, but often, the decisions and desires of Kashmiris themselves. To this end, two chapters discuss poems that channel public anger or document public hope, and a third reflects upon the capacity of poetry to thicken and complicate our understanding of the political and personal trauma that has marked the last two decades of life in Kashmir.

These poems are not offered as representative of the enormous volumes of poetry being written and sung in these years. I chose them because each of them engages, in direct or mediated ways, with the conflict. There are many more: this is a selection, and, like any selection, limited. While many of Kashmir's best-known poets write in Urdu ("Corpse" is the only Urdu poem included here) I decided to focus on poems written in the vernacular (Kashmiri) rather than in the official tongue (Urdu). Kashmiri possesses an intimacy of idiom, a fusion of the colloquial and the literary, that I found particularly attractive. I have learned enormously from these poems, and it is in that spirit that I offer them to readers. These are the voices that linger after political debates are exhausted and after the shots have been fired and bodies broken. They speak of loss, of anger, of betrayal and compromise, of the ugliness of this time, but even at their most distraught, lines and phrases in them haunt and move as they look toward a future more egalitarian, more democratic, and more humane, than the past and the present. We will do well to read, and to listen.

....

A word on these translations: attempting them might have been a quixotic enterprise simply because my Kashmiri is poor, and while I can (slowly and laboriously!) read *nastaʿliq*, the Perso-Arabic script used for Urdu and Kashmiri, the extra vowel markers used in the latter represent a challenge. The quixotic became real because of an extraordinary group of collaborators whose expertise and willingness made possible these translations: Nasir Hussain, who did much of the early work of collection and transcription and joined me in initial translations. (He found many of these poems in *Sheeraza*, the Kashmiri literary magazine published by the Jammu and Kashmir Academy of Art, Culture, and Languages—it still remains surprising to me that an "official" journal published, without any editorial comment, so many poems of protest, anger, mourning, and loss). Aijaz Hussain, Parvaiz Bukhari, Arif Ayaz Parrey, Fayaz Ahmed Dar, Idrees Kanth, Gowhar Fazili, and Inder Salim went over drafts, in some cases more than once. Members of my family pitched in: Usha Kak, Urvi Puri, and Kaushalya Kaul clarified for me the register of phrases and images as they ranged from the demotic to the literary. Many thanks to each of them. At a crucial moment, Suvaid Yaseen put his shoulder to this wheel and moved along a stuck cart, including by calling on his father's expertise! Finally, I was lucky to be in touch with Arvind Gigoo, professor and translator of poetry, whose selfless generosity and kindness to someone he has never met brought these translations to a finish.

Arif Ayaz Parrey transliterated Kashmiri poems into Roman, a difficult task, and one for which I am especially grateful.

Sadaf Munshi took time off from her own work to read with great care the transliteration and translations. She corrected errors, recommended changes, and alerted me to inappropriate turns of phrase. My gratitude for her commitment to this project. I have similar thanks to offer to Ather Zia, anthropologist and poet, for her editorial expertise.

I should say that these acts of collaboration made these poems come alive in ways that I could not anticipate. It is no exaggeration to say that these conversations allowed me to enter into the intellectual and emotional life of Kashmir in ways that were otherwise not feasible. Read, talk, and discuss, that is what we did: Why would the poet choose to write a particular form or indeed swerve away from its expectations? Why would she choose this or the other startling image or turn of phrase? What do these poems tell us about the ways in which conflict and suffering have been imagined? Answering these and ancillary questions led us into intense and sometimes very personal accounts of life under pressure. The poems did their work and more as they demanded of us a full engagement with their claims and effects.

But that is not all: once I began to reach out to poets to ask their permission to translate and publish their work, I was not prepared for the outpouring of affection that greeted me. Rather than listen to my thanks, so many poets thanked me, and I was reminded of the passion with which they mourn the shared culture of *Kashmiriyat*. I will quote only one of them: "Thanks a lot for your love towards my poetry. It must be our common pain which I have attempted to describe in my mother tongue," wrote Zahid Mukhtar *sahib*. That is the power of the poet, to remind even those who have only partial access to a shared tongue that it is a common pain that is spoken, that political and religious divides must not be allowed to sunder a common heritage. To all of these poets—eloquent spokespeople of a calamitous time—I offer my gratitude, and my hope that their work will continue to speak powerfully to all those who suffer and strive for better times.

....

Some readers will notice that the title of this volume derives from a phrase in Oliver Goldsmith's poem *The Deserted Village* (1770). Goldsmith wrote this poem to protest the dispossession of rural communities in Ireland and England by wealthy landowners who developed their country estates and manor houses by enclosing village commons and other agricultural lands. "The country blooms—a garden, and a grave," wrote Goldsmith, the alliteration emphasizing his desperate plea for public attention. For very different reasons, that dispossession is true of Kashmir today, blooming as it is with gardens and graves.

NOTES

1. For a moving account of shared lives in Kashmir, see Raina 2014.

2. The All Parties Hurriyat Conference is the umbrella organization for "separatist" political parties; they are however not united in their understanding of the territorial aims, political methods or even religious motivations of the *tehreek* and have, since the formation of the Conference in 1993, split into three factions (the most recent split took place in January 2014).

3. In early September 2014, shortly before this book went into production, terrible floods wrecked communities and towns in the Kashmir valley, including Srinagar. The civilian administration collapsed, and rescue efforts were mounted by the armed forces,

which possess both the manpower and the technological resources to deal with such calamity, and by local groups of volunteers and neighbors who helped one another with whatever resources they had at hand. As ferocious as the floodwaters themselves were the political polarizations that became visible immediately. In remarkably ugly demonstrations of predatory nationalism, news anchors from Delhi swooped down on vulnerable Kashmiris to demand that they avow their debt to the soldiers who rescued them, weren't they glad for the army now, they asked? In quick response, locals pointed out that the soldiers were only following orders, as they did when they acted against Kashmiri civilians, and that in any case the army had first evacuated the well-connected and the powerful, and only then had turned their attention to others. As I noted earlier, Kashmiri disenchantment with Indian power, and Indian resentment of Kashmiri "ingratitude," remain close to the surface.

4. Original in Urdu. Published in *Kashmir Uzma* (weekly, published from Srinagar), December 20–26, 2004.

Arjan Dev "Majboor"

Kasheer

darat yath kāri thādi sangar karān rāch
tatī chi śīnu' tạli vọpdān kuli mạch

miạtsā yath Śiv tu' Śankar chī banāvān
butu'j yọs pōś pānas pavzi lāgān

pathu'r yath rang hāitu' bạdi chi arpan
sọndar āran chu lāgith cāndi vardan

sọmiạts yath kēro nīlam chu nērān
sọmiạts yọs pȳṭh ḍȳkas kạśiri chi śērān

fizā yath śītu' jāruk pōṭ chạvith
nivān sādan reśan yus vargu'lạvith

pakān yeti yū'ri trāvān chay Vitastā
vachas mọlu' vu'ni Kạśīrē mọkhtu' mālā

chanā that Harmọkhu'c thadi pāyi naẓrā
chu lāsan manz palan prath jāyi dasgāh

pakān yath giyānoirfānu'ki chi dạriyāv
Śivas mīlith śkhu'thi tūruk chu pạrāv

vazān yeti tāru' santūras rabābas
chu milu'vith māchtay mạdrēr ābas

qalam yath Kalhanun tạrīkh lēkhān
Ghani yath krālu' pan hȳth śār śērān

vuchān khābas andar yeti Śiv chu Mardān
vanan tsūri sọnzal mas chi pạrān

sọ miạts yath sōmras bēran chu prēḍān
sọ dạrtī darśanas duniyā chu phērān

Arjan Dev "Majboor"

Kasheer

This land that high mountains protect
There, under the snows, tree sap forms

This earth which Shiva and Shankar keep making
This idol whose flowers offer themselves for worship

This soil consecrated with hundreds of colors
Beautiful rivulets adorned in silver

This soil which yields saffron and sapphire
This soil which on their foreheads Kashmiris decorate

This climate that wears a frozen-cape
Which lures away ascetics and saints

Streaming here, flowing away, the Vitasta—
The pearl necklace rich on the bosom of Kashmir

Does it not have upon it Harmukh's gaze from on high?
In this jeweled land, everywhere are nurtured dargahs

Here flow rivers of knowledge and insight[1]
Shiva gains Shakti here: such is its beauty

Here resonate the strings of the santoor and rubab
Mixed are honey and sugar in the water

Of this Kalhana's pen writes history[2]
Ghani uses his potter's string to finish couplets[3]

Here Mardan sees Shiva in his dream[4]
In forests hidden, the sonzal flower arranges her hair

This soil where nectar drips from runnels
This earth for whose darshan[5] the world wanders

amā tath miāni dạrtī śāph kạmi diut
thạlith vājin tu' dọkh sanstāp kạmi diut

kọlan manz khūni ādam kạmi sanā vōl
sọndar buth māji sānē kạmi sanā zōl

vanan manz vigni vanvun kot sanā gav
havā ḍalvun tu' mọlu'vun kot sanā gav

natsun phērun asun tay zero bam rōv
gŷvun sīran sanun dam kham panun rōv

amā hoṭ kạmi chu tsoṭmut bōlbōśas
chu moṭhmut ādu'nuk sreh prath manōśas

ḍaban pŷṭh jānu'vāran kānh nu' māzān
kukil gūgū karān poz kānh nu' bōzān

ajīb dihi chi śōlān āsmānas
magar sạrī mọhar kạri kạri dahānas

mazāran manz gabar az tandli sạvith
ghanīmāh kus yiman gōmut chu mạrith

yapạrim bālu' hālu'c kath ma sạ kar
dazān nāras andar kami ḥālu' nadhar

amā kar beyi gatshan bēdār Kạśiri
balan chọkh kar malan bulghār Kạśiri

O friend, who cursed this my earth,
Tore it down, who gave us pain and sadness?

Who sheds the blood of man into flowing rivulets
The pretty face of our mother, who burns?

In forests, the songs of fairies, where have they gone
The breeze, flowing and precious, where has it gone?

Dancing, wandering, laughing, melodies are lost
Singing, sharing secrets, our comings-and-goings, are lost

My friend, who slit the throat of speech and sounds?
Every man has forgotten youthful bonds

On balconies no one attends to the birds
The cuckoo gurgles its song, but no one hears the truth

Strange smoke smoulders across the skies
But all have sealed and sealed their mouths

In graveyards today dear ones are put to sleep in piles
Which enemy has left after killing them

Of matters on this side of the mountains, don't even ask
Burning in fires, in such a state, lost birds

O friend, when will they awake again, the Kashmiris
Wounds will heal, when will they apply balm, the Kashmiris?

·················

Published in *Sheeraza* (Kashmiri) 30:6 (1996), 66–68.

Arjan Dev Kaul "Majboor" (1924–2010) was born in Zainpora, Pulwama. He wrote poetry, short stories, and criticism in Kashmiri and Urdu. He also translated Kālidāsa's *Meghadūta* into Kashmiri and the Nilmata Purana into Urdu. He worked as a journalist for several years before becoming a teacher with the state Education Department.

NOTES

1. The poet uses the terms *gyan* and *irfan* to invoke Hindu and Islamic traditions of knowledge.

2. Kalhana's *Rajatarangini*, composed in the middle of the twelfth century, is the earliest and best-known chronicle of ancient Kashmir.

3. Mulla Tahir Ghani, better known as Ghani Kashmiri, wrote poetry in Persian in the seventeenth century. The Iranian poet Sa'ib is said to have not been able to understand Ghani's use of the Kashmiri term *kraal pan*—the string a potter uses to cut his pottery off the wheel—and thus decided to travel to Kashmir to meet Ghani, whose verses he much admired.

4. The Afghan general Ali Mardan Khan, who was appointed governor of Kashmir by Shah Jahan in 1638, saw a vision of Shiva in the mountains there and wrote a poem of praise in Persian. This poem continues to be sung in some Pandit ceremonials.

5. *Darshan* (an idea important to Hindu religious practice) is a complex form of seeing: the worshipper or seeker gazes upon the sacred object in the faith that it will reveal or manifest its divinity.

Police and paramilitary patrol during curfew in Maisuma | Srinagar, March 2013

Ghulam Hassan "Taskeen"

Nazm

Ānu' ḍabi hundi jānvārō
Bōlbōśas govuy kajar
Ḍōlmut panu'nī magangī
Khōlmut kạmi phāsi chukh

.....

Nāru' lamkav nālu'mot śahras korukh
Mạhlu' khānan cūnu' gachsu'y du'h vuzān
Vuch gọlābas āru'dali hund rang gomut
Mōsman kạmi bēvajah rāth lāy kạr
Hāvsan aḍu'vāni mọchi mūran kạru'kh

Ānu' ḍabi hu'ndi jānvārō
Hōś kar
Zahri almāsā tse khion
Poz mọkhtu' rạngi
Śah hẙnas lamu' lam
Tse yẙth fizhas andar
Ānu' ḍabi gạndhay kalāyas pẙṭh kalāy
Ānu' ḍabi hu'ndi jānvārō
Cāni bāpath
Ābu' phērẙn log ḥisāb
Khūni ādam cārsō yas pẙṭh chu ām
Vāś zan kaḍhakh pakhan
Kath kun kaḍakh

Cōn duniyā hōnzu' kiō rāday tshọṭān
Cōn akh akh tsiuh tse kiut bāri girān

Ghulam Hassan "Taskeen"

Nazm

O bird of the mirror box
Your calls have become dumb.
Deluded in your whimsy—
Who hoisted you to the gallows?

.....

Waves of flames have drawn the city into its embrace,
Smoke billows from shining grand buildings.
See, the rose's color has paled.
Who thrashes the innocent without reason?
Desires interrupted mid-way, crushed by fists.

O bird of the mirror box
Beware!
You alone have to consume poison-of-diamond
The colour of true pearl.
Breathing is strained
For you in this climate
Your mirror box has been plated and layered.
O bird of the mirror box
For you
Even drops of water were accounted for
The killing of man in the public square is common
If you were to spread your wings
In which direction will you do so?
The length and breadth of your world are shrinking
Your every moment is, for you, a great burden

Published in *Sheeraza* (Kashmiri) 27:2 (1993), 106.

Ghulam Hassan "Taskeen" was born in 1943 in Hajin Sonawari, Bandipora. He has an MA in Kashmiri from Kashmir University. He taught Kashmiri in the Government Higher Secondary School, Sumbal Sonawari and retired as headmaster from Hajin Sonawari Higher Secondary School. He writes short stories and poetry and has translated the *Gulistan-e-Saadi* into Kashmiri.

A woman mourns in front of her home, gutted by fire | Frisian Pahalgam,
November 2012

Brij Nath "Betaab"

Ghazal

Vāy pholu' nā vāri manz gul prāṇi pāṭhi
Dāri pẙṭh biūṭh picni bulbul prāṇi pāṭhi

Gāmu' vārẙn māsa āru'mi bāg gov
Kānh mangān chā hāku' krēnjul prāṇi pāṭhi

Gūri vānas pẙṭh samān chā gāmu' śuri
Rẙtsh kaṛān chā kāṇsi 'vārul' prāṇi pāṭhi

Kānh mangān chā az ti hamsāyan gurus
Kānh anān chā gāv kiuth ḍul prāṇi pāṭhi

Noṣi yivān chā az ti mālini pyāv hẙth
Kuni garān chā chān manzul prāṇi pāṭhi

Patji pẙṭh chādāni hokhnāvān voṇi
Chā bẙṭān kuni kanz tu' muhul prāṇi pāṭhi

Dosu' divān dārith tithay kāṇi az ti chā
Śuri khẙvān chā tsūri śahtul prāṇi pāṭhi

Vẙthu' baṭhẙn pẙṭh kānh karān chā īz rōv
Kānh vasān chā nāvi Tulmul prāṇi pāṭhi

Akh ākis kāṭsāh karav āsi pāmū'pām
Kyāhsa hē asi sapdinā miul prāṇi pāṭhi

Phēri garu' Bētāb yeli Āfāq Azīz
Sōzi śech bẙnu' nov longun tul prāṇi pāṭhi

Brij Nath "Betaab"

Ghazal

Ah! Will not the flower bloom in the garden as in the past?
Does the bulbul perch on the window-sill to sing, as in the past?

Have our village gardens been turned into market-gardens yet?
Does no one ask for a basketful of greens, as in the past?

Do the village children still gather at the milkman's store?
Do they still invent nicknames—*sparrowhawk*—as in the past?

Does anyone come asking neighbours for *gurus*?[1]
Does anyone bring the cow a *dul*,[2] as in the past?

Does daughter-in-law still bring birth-gifts from her mother's house?
Does the carpenter craft—anywhere?—a cradle, as in the past?

Is grain still dried on plain straw-mats?
Is the mortar-and-pestle found anywhere, as in the past?

Are mud-walls felled the same way even today?[3]
Do children eat mulberry in hiding, as in the past?

Does anyone sing and dance on the Vyeth's banks on Eid?
Does anyone boat down to Tulla-Mulla, as in the past?

How much are we going to taunt each other?
Do you think we'll never come together, as in the past?

Betaab says he will return home when Afaq Aziz
Sends word that Sister picks up a new *longun*,[4] as in the past.

....

Published in *Naghma te Beath* (*Musical Songs*), compiled and edited Dr Afaq Aziz (Srinagar: Writers Organization for Research and Development, 2003), 108–9.

Brij Nath Watal "Betaab" was born in 1953 in Akingam, Anantnag. He studied at the Amar Singh College, Srinagar. He writes poetry in Kashmiri and Urdu and has been an advisor to the Jammu and Kashmir Academy of Art, Culture and Languages. He has worked as a broadcaster and journalist for All India Radio.

NOTES

1. *gurus* is whey, the liquid that separates when butter is churned from milk. Here, the whey that is shared indicates not only neigbborliness but an organic life where little goes to waste.

2. *dul* is a clay basin; the act of feeding each cow from a *dul* suggests intimacy and respect.

3. a *dossa* is a mud-wall; it crumbles when children clamber on it to steal fruit.

4. *longun* is an archaic term: it refers to a large (1 seer) measure for rice. Its use suggests a renewed and generous welcome for guests and family. However, this line can be translated differently, for *tule longun* is also a game played by little girls. The line will then read: "Sends word that sisters are playing *tule longun*, as in the past." My commentary on this poem in the chapter "The Witness of Poetry" makes clear my reasons for preferring the first translation.

Funeral procession of Qazi Zubair, a militant commander | Keller Shopian,
May 2011

Ghulam Nabi Tak "Naazir"

Ghazal

Yinu' āv vanu'nay tī tī van
Thav thav līkhith bād kathan

Pakhu' phuci vāvas sarirah pio
Rāvmit ālav tsọn tarfan

Tim kot gạy yim ạsī gaṇḍān
Gọni gāmu'ts ạisi dastāran

Lāśan pỷth chu nu' līkhith kenh
Phiur logmut beyi tasvīran

Tshāyav bebi manz roch kenhtām
ạchithop thōvmut dith gāśan

Yī yōt bōzān gov yạtskāl
Vani chinu' gatsnu'y ṭās kanan

Lōg zamānan ādu'mi khāv
Vātānu'y chinu' kun rasman

Gāb haraf gạy rakhnu'y tal
Vọlu' von dimu' hav insānan

Vāṇij vāṇij zan dubu' phīr
Ạchi lạj mājan hu'nz gobran

Teli ōs aki chiki nab vọślān
Az ratu' sạri buthi akhbāran

Vatu' chiv tohi kati kati tshāṇḍān
Az chav vatu' prỷth śāyi dafan

Tāpu' tekỷn gạy khām tamah
Ku'tsnay chā vuni kānh dāman

Ghulam Nabi Tak "Naazir"

Ghazal

That which could not be told, tell it now
Keep, keep writing, the value of speech

Wings broken, the wind falls helpless
In all directions, calls are lost

Where have they gone, they who used to tie
Our turbans are now crumpled[1]

There is nothing written on corpses
The pictures are shuffled once again

Shadows have bred something in their laps
The light has blindfolded itself

All this while, this is what we have been hearing
Our ears no longer hear any bangs

The times have turned man-eating
Caught up in rituals we get nowhere

Letters have disappeared under lines
Come now, let's look for human beings

Heart after heart as if turned upside down
The evil eye—of mothers!—blights beloved sons

Then, a single drop would redden the sky[2]
Today, newspapers are headlined in blood

Where do you go to seek for paths
Today, paths are entombed everywhere

Spots of sunshine were but false allure
Is there any hem not yet wet

Bōzav and kar vāti kitāb
Trảvyā ạsi vuni tamhīdan?

Tārakh vālukh Naazir bọn
Natu' kus kari grỷnd ratu' katran?

We'll see when the book will end
Are we done with the preface now?

Bring down the stars, *Naazir*
Else who will count the drops of blood?

···················

Published in *Sheeraza* (Kashmiri) 29:4 (1994), 66. Also published in Ghulam Nabi 'Naazir,' *Reh Te Rood* (Srinagar, 2005), 75–76.

Ghulam Nabi Tak "Naazir" was born in 1935 in Yaripora, Kulgam. He has advanced degrees in Kashmiri and Urdu and was employed by the government. He has published thirty-five books, three of which have been awarded prizes by the Jammu and Kashmir Cultural Academy: *Hiya Gond* (1979), *Rav te Rotul* (1983) and *Acchre Tsangi* (1991).

NOTES

1. This couplet refers to the loss of the Pandits, identified by the turbans (dastaar) they tied, particularly on ceremonial occasions.

2. This refers to the belief that the sky reddens when someone dies—now, the shedding of blood has no such effect.

Shabir "Azar"

Corpse

In the mirror of that lake,
what should I see . . . ?

from its depths
that stranger-like corpse
stares

I have often
thrown a stone—
I wished to smash that mirror

ripples formed, spread, dissipated

and

at the furthest reaches of the silent lake
the same corpse kept staring

the corpse!

as if it would steal
my musings today . . . !
or
fold the imprint of my future
into the vastness of the lake!

Why should I pick up a stone
and smash this mirror

if the corpse
is in the lake
the lake too
is in the corpse

or

both are locked in drops of
water . . . !

....

Original in Urdu. Published in *Kashmir Uzma* (weekly, published from Srinagar), December 20–26, 2004.

Shabir "Azar" (1963–2012) was born in Gund Khwaja Qasim, Pattan, Baramula. He attended the local government school, received his BA from Bemina College, Srinagar and later an MA in Urdu. He worked in the state Health Department. His poems have been published in a volume titled *Sareer-e-Qalam.*

Villagers return from the funeral of Bilal Ahmed Sheikh, killed in a shooting by
government forces | Singhpora Baramulla, August 2010

An army soldier frisks a villager during a cordon-and-search operation | Tral
Pulwama, May 2013

A woman confronts paramilitary soldiers during a protest against the killing of a school boy, Inayat Khan | Srinagar, January 2010

Visiting Kashmir, Re-learning Kashmir

I did not live in Kashmir, but it was certainly home when we visited. My father and mother grew up there, and both sets of grandparents had identical homes, built on a shared plot. So Srinagar was home to our family, even though my father worked in Bengal and we lived there. I grew up thinking of myself as Kashmiri, and if I could barely speak the language, I certainly made up for that lack by my devotion to the food. As a child, and even as I grew into adulthood and a more political understanding of personal and collective identity, I saw no contradiction between being Indian and being Kashmiri, in the same way as my friends were simultaneously Indian and Punjabi or Indian and Tamilian. Throughout the 1970s, on all our visits, nothing in Srinagar suggested a divide between the two, or at least not to me. I was aware that when my grandmother spoke of us, she said we lived in India, but I was happy to gloss that dissonance by thinking of it as the quaint result of her disappointment that both her sons had professional jobs far away from home! Both my grandfathers taught in Srinagar colleges, which meant that the city, and particularly the shopping areas, seemed populated by their students, which made walking with them a perpetual human obstacle course. They were stopped all the time as people greeted them, and then I was introduced. Their social centrality rubbed off on us visiting grandchildren: people we did not know recognized us, and we felt we belonged. (In our extended family, only two sets of cousins lived in Srinagar; the majority of us lived elsewhere in India).

As I grew older and began to learn the history of the erstwhile princely state of Jammu and Kashmir, some of the fissures between Kashmir and

India became visible. In 1947, as plans were made for the end of British rule, the British had recommended that each "princely state" accede to either Pakistan or India. The future was clear for most of the princely states— even as the rulers of these states were offered a notional choice between the new nations, there was little doubt that each princely state would be incorporated into the national landmass that surrounded it. Because Jammu and Kashmir shared boundaries with both India and Pakistan and had a majority Muslim population with sizeable Hindu and Buddhist populations, it represented a particular challenge. Leaders of both the Muslim League and the Congress had lobbied Maharaja Hari Singh to join Pakistan and India, respectively, but he delayed his decision, hoping perhaps to rule an independent kingdom, or certainly to avoid becoming a part of Pakistan. If the principles supposedly applied by Cyril Radcliffe and the Boundary Commission to the determination of the boundaries of India and Pakistan had been extended to this princely state, then either the entire state, being Muslim-majority, should have gone to Pakistan or, if the unit of division was to be the district, then Muslim-majority border districts and contiguous territories should have become Pakistani. In any case Hari Singh's rule was threatened by people's movements for democracy; the "Quit Kashmir" slogan directed against his authority by Sheikh Abdullah and the All Jammu and Kashmir National Conference echoed the "Quit India" slogan directed against the British by the Indian National Congress. All this political activity became moot with the entry of Pakistani-sponsored raiders, whose brief success caused the fearful maharaja to accede to India as the price for Indian troops entering the fray. Fifteen months later, after India and Pakistan fought their first war, Jammu and Kashmir ended up messily divided: the valley of Kashmir, Jammu, and Ladakh came under Indian control; territories west and north of them, including Gilgit and Baltistan, were under Pakistani domination. In response to the unusual circumstances by which it acquired this territory, India sought to guarantee a special status for Jammu and Kashmir via Article 370 of the Constitution, which allowed for substantial forms of autonomy. Further, in a gesture designed for international consumption, India promised a plebiscite that would, when the time was right, determine the state's future.

For thirty years and more, elections in Indian Kashmir were manipulated by New Delhi and its local collaborators; politicians deemed pro-Pakistani were unelectable. But those lines were uncertain; after all, when in 1953 Sheikh Abdullah explored the possibilities of a more independent politics, or even when he emphasized the possibilities made available by Article 370, he was arrested, and was to spend twenty years in jail. Relations between the central and state governments developed along predictable lines: New Delhi's priority was the massive security apparatus that ringed the state, ostensibly to protect India from Pakistani and Chinese attack. In practice however, that apparatus—large swathes of militarized territories, entire districts where the army or the Border Security Force is law, the building of massive cantonments that restructured local agricultural and trading practices, and lines of control that isolate communities from each other—was turned against Kashmiris even more than it addressed developments across borders. All else became secondary, and as Indo-Pakistani (and Indo-Chinese) relations degenerated into repeated wars, whatever little constitutionally feasible political autonomy was imagined for and by Kashmiris became a threat to the absolute authority of an increasingly militarized state.

The massively rigged elections of 1987 were a turning point, and made clear to a new generation of educated and politicized voters that the electoral process would continue to be manipulated to suppress candidates who were not pro-India. At the same time, the *mujahideen* in Afghanistan were gaining in their insurgency against the Soviet occupation forces— their example, and the support they had garnered from Pakistan, led thousands of Kashmiri young men, now organized into a motley collection of insurgent groups, to take on the Indian military, paramilitary, and state police forces. The 1990s saw Kashmir spiraling into a vortex of violence; large sections of the population, notably Kashmiri Hindus from the valley, were displaced and exiled; tens of thousands, militants, civilians, and some troops, were killed. These years polarized Kashmiris as never before: governance became the playground of intelligence and security agencies, and the basic trust and goodwill and tolerance that allow societies to cohere were systematically eroded. As all semblances of civil society and everyday comfort disappeared, destroyed by militants as well as the government forces who fought them, Kashmir became uninhabitable for many people. My parents, who had moved to Srinagar after my father's retirement, began living in Delhi through the year, though my father visited for short periods in subsequent years. In effect, we shut down our home, with a caretaker living in the outhouse.

For an Indian Kashmiri like me, now living in the United States, the violence and rapidity of events in Kashmir beggared any explanations we might offer. One set of our relatives continued to live in Kashmir over the summers and move to Delhi for the winter. But they too had stories of attempted kidnappings (of both Hindus and Muslims, of course), the destruction of communities large and small, and everyday fear, and so our Kashmir—at a distance—became a battleground of family opinions too. As with most Indians, the largest number of them believed that the state must crack down on militants, especially those who fought in the name of Islam or Pakistan and thus denied the secular character of India as well as the tolerance and ease of *Kashmiriyat* (a word that was used more and more as its claims for Muslim and Hindu coexistence appeared increasingly tenuous). But there were those who said that they thought this mess was the product of decades of undemocratic and coercive governance, and who pointed to the many Indian military and paramilitary officers and bureaucrats who left Kashmir enriched by their stints in authority there, as well as the corruption endemic in all agencies of the state.

In summer 2003, with the militancy seemingly now contained, our family went home to Srinagar. The calendars in our house stood frozen at October 1999, which was the last month anyone had lived there. We had feared great damage to the house in the intervening years, but were relieved to find only enormous volumes of dust, and the detritus of pigeons nesting in the attic, encouraged by broken windowpanes. As we cleaned, the hard work being done by two neighborhood caretakers, Abdul Gaffar and Raghunath, it was tempting to think of the restoration of this home as a metaphor for a renewed Kashmir, and a return to a functional, multireligious, syncretic culture.

However, it was clear that any such restoration was going to be hard, if not impossible, to achieve. The brutal history of the past fourteen years could not be wished away: Kashmiris were now a people ground down under the military might of the state and the violence of well-armed militants. It was also clear that the state of siege in the valley was not going to be lifted any day soon. Conversations in Srinagar always boiled down to this: too many people had enriched themselves in the last decade, and they had a great deal to lose if the conflict in Kashmir de-escalated. Stories were rife of the wealth accrued by the leaders of each of many political factions. Similar stories circulated about bureaucrats, officers of army units and of each paramilitary force (their acronyms—BSF, CRPF, SSB, JKP, RR, STF—had become the new idiom of the Kashmiri language). People talked at length of the money that circulated in the valley via each of these groups and their counterparts in Pakistan, and of how much the politico-military elite on both sides of the border benefited from the state of affairs in Kashmir.

For a visitor like me, there was something more that was deeply upsetting, that is, the heady power of this elite bull-dozing its way in elaborate convoys past locals who learned to step aside or be assaulted. The local papers described a woman professor whose car failed to give way quickly enough to an official car being dragged out by her hair and beaten. I saw officers and their families go shopping on Residency Road or Lambert Lane, with trucks of soldiers deployed on either side, all in addition to the forces permanently on patrol there. Local Kashmiris had learned to ignore such activities as the antics of the powerful, but for the likes of us, every day offered ugly instances of the ways of a superior occupying force. The boulevard that fringes the Dal Lake was alive with people, but no one could take free passage for granted, for at a moment's notice the road was blocked and civilians made to detour. Perhaps most egregious of all was the fact that local, non-upper class Kashmiris were turned away from the springs at Chashmashahi, while outsiders were granted access.

There were other concerns: older Kashmir Hindu practices and shrines were being remade by the paramilitaries guarding them. The Kheer Bhawani Temple in the village of Tula Mula and the Shankaracharya Temple that overlooks Srinagar, once serene and calm, were now armed camps, festooned with the bright colors and signboards so beloved by military officers. Commanding officers of units stationed at these sites had turned them into advertisements for themselves—now you could only get to the Devi via CRPF yellow and red, and by walking past painted slogans alien to Kashmiri Hindus. When we visited, bhajans that blare during *jagrans* in Delhi played loudly; only the wonderful old chinars suggested all that was once distinctively Kashmiri about *Tulla Mulla*. A Ram Mandir was being built at the site of the ancient sun temple at Martand (Mattan), and seemed a deliberate refashioning of local Hindu worship to obey the dictates of Hindutva practice. But worst of all were the excessive displays put on for the benefit of Amarnath yatris (and which actually function as a warning to local Kashmiris). Along the route past Pahalgam, and to some extent on the Baltal route, CRPF- and BSF- (and occasionally, J&K Police) sponsored banners and wall slogans welcomed yatris. These units made available tea and snacks, and announced them as *prasad*.

Still, this was a summer of comparative peace, and everywhere in the valley people celebrated their opportunity to travel to places that they have not dared to visit for years. An entire generation deprived of civic life and of the joys of Kashmir now flocked to Pahalgam and Gulmarg, and the Mughal Gardens were full of local visitors. No one knew how long this lull would last, and locals were moved by a near-hysterical urge to wander, to picnic, to talk of the future. This seemed a moment of hope, of young people wishing for a life different from that they have suffered so far, of conversations in which plans are made for a Kashmir in which ideas can flourish, the mind can be without fear, and the head can be held high. I thought of Rabindranath Tagore's great nationalist poem, "Where the Mind Is Without Fear," for its aspirations—as true for Kashmiris as for Indians more generally—were those of the young as they imagined again a life outside of the machinations of international politics, paramilitary strategies, and the self-aggrandizement of those who rule Kashmir.

....

My visits continue, and there are times when matters seem calmer, but it is also clear none of the underlying political problems have been resolved. In August 2008, for instance, there are days when the tourists are crowding through the markets in Srinagar, and even locals manifest a palpable pleasure in summer activities, but the atmosphere remains strained. I will here record a memory (I should note that such remembrance is crucial to making clear my own relation, as part outsider and part insider, to the situation in Kashmir). I am walking in the Polo View market in central Srinagar with my mother. She wears a sari, and thus, even though I wear a beard, it is clear to all those who see us that we are Hindu. This means that the Indian paramilitary forces, who are now deployed by the central government in Kashmir, view us benignly, unlike their response to other locals; it also means that their body language is far less threatening, and indeed threatened, as we approach. One of the stores we walk past has the family of an officer of the Central Reserve Police Force (CRPF) visiting—

there is a CRPF van outside, and a small group of soldiers have fanned out around the store. We come closer and I see that there is a little girl, no more than six or seven years old, standing between one soldier and his automatic rifle, insistently grabbing it (he resists, but mildly, which tells me that she must be the daughter of the officer in the store). We reach the store just at the moment when the girl begins placing her hand on the trigger guard as she pretends that she is in fact wielding the weapon. I decide to intervene and ask, in Hindi, why the soldier is allowing her to play with what is a dangerous weapon; what if something goes wrong? What can I do, he says, she doesn't listen . . . he says no more, knowing that I, visibly a member of the "officer class" myself, will understand the dynamic at work. The little girl, hearing my question, slips away into the store, and I step aside too, and stand alongside an old man sitting by the store entrance. He wears the skullcap Kashmiri Muslim artisans often wear, and his beard is white and tidy. He is the owner whose son now runs the store, and he has long known my family. He has been watching all this while, and now his face wears a look of gentle bemusement. He says nothing, but there is no mistaking the look in his weary eyes: you can speak, they say, you can do the sensible thing, you have the right to intervene—you are Hindu, clearly upper class, and speak Hindi with a non-Kashmiri accent. The soldier is trained to respond to you differently from the way he responds to me; he is your creature, and hence yours to question or to shame.

The ironies multiply: even as most Pandits have left Kashmir, occasions like this one made me feel oddly privileged, as it was clear to me that my right to question the soldier came from my being a Hindu who spoke Hindi with an "Indian" accent.

....

In conversations with friends and neighbors, I feel acutely their loss of trust in India. Few of those I spend time with speak directly about their political desires, but they all talk intensely about life in the last two decades. Listening to them is to drown, slowly but surely, in a sea of stories. It was impossible to avoid them, for like the legendary lakes that dot Kashmir's valleys, these stories were everywhere. I will re-tell some stories here to suggest one powerful reason why, in the midst of seeming calm and teeming tourists, an administrative decision about land usage on the Amarnath yatra route precipitated a massive crisis.[1] The issue was not simply that of land, but of a land so drenched in tales of suffering and violence that peace is never more than surface thin.

There is the story that begins as the snowmelt from the high mountains, which each year swells the streams, rivers, and lakes, and brings life to paddy fields and vegetable gardens. For the past nineteen years, this rush of water has featured strange new fruit—bodies and faces—mangled or sometimes oddly preserved, as they bob along the surface. No Kashmiri who watches them pass by, or sees them being pulled to the side, forgets what they have seen. These visions sear themselves into the brain, and the only comfort is to tell of what they have seen, till the vision itself, and the tone of the story, becomes muted, and matter-of-fact.

There is the story of the Gujjar girl, raped by three paramilitary soldiers, and left to die in the fields. She lived, the three were prosecuted, and perhaps punished, but the story does not end with this intimation of justice, for the restless storyteller still wonders why no one asked about the seventeen other soldiers who watched and did nothing? Should they not have intervened, for were they not in uniform, and supposed to be protecting their own, their fellow-citizens of the republic?

Then there is a tale with many variations: two brothers, on their way to till their fields, meet a contingent of soldiers. The soldiers demand that the brothers show them the route up a hillside, and then, when they are near the top, tell them to stand by the lip of the river gorge. How many brothers are you at home, they ask. Four say the brothers. Good, says one of the soldiers, then we can kill the two of you and there will still be two others. This will be good population control but your families will survive. They tell them to raise their *pherans* and cover their faces. Two shots ring out, both bodies plummet into the gorge. The younger one dies, but the older lives, as the shot enters one cheek and exits the other, shattering one side of his face. Their village below hears the shots, and then sees, in the stream, the red of blood. This story too is told without flourishes, for the teller knows that even as he tells the story of his best friend, the younger brother who was murdered, he can claim no unique pain, for there are so many more stories like this one.

There are stories that feature Papa 1 and Papa 2, the notorious interrogation centers in the heart of posh Srinagar. Many died there, or were mangled in mind and body, and some claim that their cries still reverberate there. These buildings are now back with the civil administration, have been refurbished, and house important officials. The administration claimed that renovation and civilian usage would heal these buildings of their histories, but the many who were interned there, and the many, many more whose loved ones disappeared into the two papas, see little healing, only a handing over of property from one set of rulers to another. This too is one effect of the circulation of such stories, for those who hear them, and have heard them for almost two decades now, cannot hear when those in power speak. They stand and listen—in their own self-conception Kashmiris have always been forced to stand and listen—but all they actually hear are the elegies of the disappeared and the dead.

Pictures tell stories too, of course, and there are so many to be seen, for the world has an insatiable appetite for images of suffering. Crying women crowd these frames, their sorrow and their anger at odds with their *chunnis* and head scarves of many colors. Their faces, and those of the little ones, who cry not because they know who has been lost but because their mothers and aunts are distraught, are the new face of Kashmir. They weep as one for their gun-toting insurgent son, who climbed the high mountains in pursuit of a dangerous dream, or their carpenter-brother, who left the house for supplies and never returned home. There are pictures of buildings aflame, the end result of a skirmish between violent men, or the more spectacular one of the precise moment when the military blows up two homes from which militants fire at them. The tone of the photograph is uncannily like the tone of the stories: the roar of the blast is muted into the visual whoosh of debris flying high, with the quiet, understated certainty of death. Pictures and poetry, stories and songs—who could have known that two decades of violence could have made these the weapons of the weak? And then there are other pictures that are as inspiring: masses of men, and of women, mobilized into processions, surging forward, arms in the air and mouths open with slogans, storming into a future that holds few promises except for the certainty of more pain.

There is another set of stories that is told less and less as the years go by, but whose power to haunt and to vex does not fade. They too feature people who were killed, but they are mostly about exile, about leaving homes and hearths in fear. These are Hindu stories, or at least stories of Hindus, and of their horror at hearing, in their neighborhoods, the strident voices of hate. These testimonials are necessary reminders that no one abandons home until forced to do so, or unless they are deeply fearful of the consequences of staying on. There is no compensation for their loss, which is also the loss of a set of stories that complemented and completed Kashmir's web of enchantments. They will never be replaced, but, slowly but surely, their telling will fade in the face of the other more urgent, more recently painful, stories Muslims have to tell.

And finally, when all the policy planners, the politicians, and the military men have done their work, it is these stories that will defy their logic. We—I now write as an Indian and a democrat—have no convincing stories to offer Kashmiris, no narratives of inclusion and oneness. We have watched, and listened (but not really done either) as large sections of "our" Kashmiri population—Muslim and Hindu—are brutalized and reduced to the status of supplicants. We think our promises of development, and of belonging to an India burgeoning into a superpower, will wean them away from the stories they now imbibe. We should know that we have in fact no stories to offer that are not hollow, corrupt, and coercive. And Kashmir is now a churning sea of stories, stories that move and mobilize, and irrigate suffering and struggle.

....

It is now summer 2010, and I visit again for a month in August. I am horrified once more at the chasm between people and the security forces, even worse than the great distrust that separates people from the government. Stone-pelting young men lead larger crowds into political agitation, and every day adds to the list of those killed or wounded by Indian troops or the J&K Police. Here, to retain a sense of the urgency of that moment, I reproduce a diary I kept between July 29 and August 3, when the situation was at its worst:

Thursday, July 29: I fly into Srinagar to visit my mother, who is spending a long summer in our family home away from the heat of Delhi. At Delhi airport, I am startled by the number of army men waiting to catch the hopper flight to Srinagar via Jammu: I had not thought that soldiers flew on commercial airlines, but there they were, their presence a foretaste of things ahead. My direct flight into Srinagar is full of Kashmiri families, many visibly settled abroad, visiting home, and several Amarnath yatris. Three of them, all young men, large *tikas* on foreheads, are thrilled when they share the bus to the airplane with four European women tourists—

they chuckle, nudge each other, and fondle themselves in sheer joy at this payoff early on their pilgrimage.

Srinagar has turned into a city of shutters. The taxi home makes quick progress as there is virtually no civilian traffic on the streets. We pass a four-vehicle army convoy—my taxi driver makes careful eye contact with the gun-toting jawan at the back of the last jeep in order to get permission to overtake. A nod in reply allows us to zoom ahead, and I make desultory conversation while reading the occasional handwritten wall slogan that says "GO INDIA GO" or the harsher "INDIAN DOGS GO BACK." That makes me an unwanted visitor, I suppose, but then, not fifteen minutes ago, as I walked to the airport prepaid taxi stand, one driver called out to his compatriot who had taken charge of me: "*Haiyo yi chui local*" ("Hey you, he is a local"). Poised between an Indian citizenship I wear with pride in my professional life abroad, and a "localness," which has learned to fear the cynical might of the Indian security apparatus, in Kashmir and elsewhere, I wonder what my time in Srinagar will bring.

Watching television in the evening reminds me of the fundamental absence of interest in the Indian media in the situation in Kashmir. Major news channels report on protests here, particularly if protestors are shot or property is damaged, but there is no attempt whatsoever to ask if these protests are a continuation of two decades of political unrest, and not simply random acts of violence instigated (as our home minister would have it, by the Lashkar-e-Taiba or some such convenient scapegoat). Last year's assembly elections, and the installation of Omar Abdullah's government, was celebrated as a reminder that Kashmiris were not alienated from Indian democracy, and thus that no political initiatives were necessary to address their demands, articulated for five decades now and supposedly guaranteed by Article 370, to define for themselves the forms of their autonomy. But the last few weeks have seen renewed protests in Kashmir, with stone pelting and demonstrations recurring in Srinagar, Sopore, Anantnag (Islamabad), and elsewhere. The military has been called out once (only a "flag march," is the official word), but the CRPF and J&K Police have fired upon and killed protestors already, and are in any case on edge in the streets. The Hurriyat announces a weekly calendar of protests, but there is widespread awareness that they no longer initiate or control these demonstrations, which seem less orchestrated and planned and more the product of rising anger among people brutalized by the daily humiliations of living under a security regime.

Television this evening also brings a reminder of the ways in which public debate within Srinagar is censored. Two channels, *Sën Channel* and *Sën Awaaz* (sën means "ours" in Kashmiri), are off the air, and the former broadcasts the headline: "The Transmission of *Sën Channel* has been Banned by Government, under order no: DMS/PS-MISC/10/840-52, Dated: 29-07-2010." I ask my mother if she knows why these channels have been banned. Her answer is succinct: they discussed local political events, covered street demonstrations, and told the truth.

Every evening at 7 PM we turn to ETV, an Urdu-language channel, to listen to their half-hour news bulletin on Kashmir. This is the fullest and most accurate account of all that happens here, and their local correspondent, Manoj Kaul, is measured in his reportage without omitting major details. Kashmiri news channels have been coerced into trimming their news bulletins into vapid coverage of government events, and it is ironic—but precisely symptomatic—that the best source of information broadcasts from Hyderabad.

In the evening, my neighborhood is preternaturally quiet, and I cannot help thinking of the silence of a mausoleum.

Friday, July 30: The authorities have banned the weekly *jumma namaz* at the main Jama Masjid, and several other large masjids, for five weeks now, and each Friday brings about a declared or undeclared curfew. Today is no different. My mother tells me that the local paper has not been delivered for several days now—it is being printed, but the deliveryman lives in Maisuma and cannot make his rounds. Maisuma is a neighborhood that has seen sustained public protests and is thus kept under virtual curfew at all times. Only government employees who carry appropriate identification and those who have curfew passes are allowed onto the streets, and even those passes are not always respected by the police or CRPF constables who patrol Srinagar's barricaded streets. Government employees have been told that they must report for duty, but the government offices in our neighborhood are more or less deserted. (Incidentally, a house close by sports a signboard that would be witty if it were not an example of the growth of high-level bureaucratic offices: Office of the Chairman, Committee for Examination of Demands for New Administrative Units.)

To my mind, these empty administrative offices represent one of the worst forms of collateral damage suffered by Kashmiris over the last two decades. An astonishing number of Kashmiri men (and some women, of course) are on government payrolls, and here I do not include the many (some estimate up to 100,000) who receive regular stipends from various intelligence agencies and secret services. Civil services and local administration have been systematically hollowed-out over the past two decades; there is virtually no accountability at any level, and receiving a government salary is tantamount to being on the dole. If nothing else, the Indian state has revenged itself on Kashmiris by teaching them how not to work while still drawing salaries. This *salariat* functions as a vast buffer between the Indian state and the elected J & K government and the mass of people whose livelihood depends on daily work and trade, and, like government servants everywhere, they constitute a bulwark against political movements that mobilize common people. Of course this is not always the case; there have been times when some sectors of government employees have taken to the streets to protest different facets of Indian rule, but they are, for the most part, at peace with their salaries.

By the evening reports of demonstrations and the shooting of protestors are confirmed: three dead (two in Sopore) and many injured, including a score wounded by bullets. It is now clear that tomorrow, a day on which the Hurriyat calendar encouraged people to resume normal activities and stock up on supplies, is going to be another day of curfews and mounting tension. There seems to be no official response other than the police action on the street; no ministers or any other government officials are on television to explain the day's events and to offer some account of plans to deescalate violence. In the absence of official explanations, rumors provide information: a substantial number of the dead and injured sustain head and chest wounds, and it seems that the security forces are shooting to kill rather than to injure or maim. Conversations about cynical politics abound: Is it possible that these street protests are not being halted because their random, unsupervised quality undercuts the Hurriyat's claim to being the political leadership of the mass of Kashmiris angry with life under military occupation? Some argue that precisely because there are no known leaders of these demonstrations, they cannot really be said to serve a partisan political purpose. Some weeks ago, a group of young men in Sopore—leaders of street action—ignored Syed Ali

Shah Geelani's call to avoid stone pelting and rejected the appeal made by Syed Salahuddin, the Pakistan-based head of the Hizb-ul-Mujahidin, to not precipitate confrontations and disruptions that will get in the way of a longer, more sustained struggle. But there is no denying that the largest mass of people respond positively to the Hurriyat calendar, and that Geelani is the man with the greatest public heft here.

I read a local English-language newspaper that, on its front page, prints in Urdu a revolutionary poem by Sahir Ludhianvi (they print it under a caption, *"Bol ki lab azad hain tere"*—"Speak, for your lips are free"—which is the first line of a protest poem by Faiz Ahmed Faiz). The final lines from Sahir's poem are worth transcribing here, for they take on an uncanny urgency in Srinagar—this most progressive Indian poet now speaks for those subject to the unthinking muscularity of the regime:

Yeh kis ka lahu hai kaun maraa
ham Thaan chuke hain ab jii meN
har zaalim se takraaeNge
tum samjhaute ki aas rakho
ham aage baRte jaenge
har manzil ae azadi ki kasam
har manzil par dohraenge
yeh kis ka lahu hai kaun maraa

Whose blood is this? Who is dead?
In our hearts we are resolved
Every tyrant we will smash
You can hope for compromise
We'll continue to stride ahead.
Each step we swear in freedom's name
Each step we'll swear again
Whose blood is this? Who is dead?

Saturday, July 31: We have a young neighbor who steps out at 5 AM every morning to see if he can buy *lavasas* or *girdas* (local bread made in a tandoor) and milk, and he does the same for us. Bakeries and other stores shut by 6 PM so that people can be home before the curfew is enforced, but today he comes back to say that the bakery has not opened. Given how wedded Kashmiris are to their *lavasas*, this is as pronounced a symptom of civic disorder as any.

The curfew, we are told, is to be enforced more closely today, but that does not seem to stop people from taking to the streets all over the valley; the list of towns and villages in which people mobilize knits together north and south Kashmir, as well as Srinagar, in a network of protest: Sopore, Pampore, Naidkhai Sumbal, Pattan, Handwara, Kupwara, Kreeri, Varmul, Bijbehara, Kakpora, Ganderbal (the chief minister's constituency). Two (or is it three?) more men are shot by the police and CRPF, many more injured, hospitals in Srinagar report a shortage of blood. The pattern of daily protest and firing is now firmly in place: people gather to raise slogans and march towards government buildings, the young throw stones, the CRPF retaliate in kind (including, in a species of collective punishment, by breaking the windows of homes in the urban areas where protestors originate), use tear gas, and then, after they fire warning shots, shoot to kill and maim.

But there are variations in these seemingly established patterns, new participants in these protests. In several instances, women are at the forefront, and we see images of young women throwing stones at the security forces. Today also sees a demonstration at Uri, which is close to the border and home to a great army presence; but mercifully, the army does not intervene as protestors make clear that their protests are not directed at them. Today also sees substantial damage to government property: a building at the Amargarh station at Sopore, police vehicles, two Air Force trucks. And where larger crowds gather, as at Kreeri, they burn a camp of the Special Operations Group (the SOG is a police auxiliary recruited locally, including surrendered militants, and is loathed because they are often used by the security services to do their dirty work for them). One story that makes the rounds—no news channel in Kashmir or elsewhere confirms this—is that two army vehicles were burnt when the soldiers in them refused their officer's order to take action against the protestors who had stopped them. We will not fire on the unarmed, they are supposed to have said.

Kashmir has never seen such widespread anger and mobilization, say those who lived through the worst episodes of armed militancy in the 1990s. Then, state forces fought those equipped to fight back, and civilian casualties (and there were many) could be blamed on insurgents and counter insurgency tactics. Now there are no armed militants, only people, their voices, and their bodies on the road, and of course there are stones. Policemen do get hurt, and isolated government officials are thrashed, but the only people who are shot are civilians. A Delhi-based news channel used the word "miscreants" to describe the protestors who burned a building, and once again I was reminded of the chasm that divides opinion-makers in Delhi and events on the ground here. Would we ever call those who marched for freedom against the British "miscreants"? Or even those who torched the police station at Chauri Chaura during the Non-cooperation Movement in 1922? (It is another matter that Gandhi called a halt to the movement in the face of that incident; but this is another time and place, and there is no Gandhi here.)

And that is an important part of the problem in Kashmir. If the British had insisted that Gandhi was not to be dealt with as a politician, that he and his politics had no *locus standi*, a different map of protest would have emerged all over India. Our home minister's line on Kashmir has been clear: emboldened perhaps by the election results in 2009, he had declared the separatists irrelevant. But they have never been that, and in fact are the only set of politicians who have consistently argued the need to re-examine Kashmir's status within the Indian Union. There are those amongst the Hurriyat who are amenable to the development of political systems in Jammu & Kashmir that will in fact put into practice the autonomy, the special status, constitutionally available to this state. There are also those who are much more independentist in their aspirations, and there are a few (and increasingly fewer) others who think of a merger with their Islamic neighbor Pakistan, if only because that was the principle of the merger of majority populations that was supposed to govern the allotment of territories during the Partition process of 1947.

Successive regimes in Delhi have sought to delegitimize this entire range of political opinion, and that has been a huge and arrogant miscalculation. Kashmiris have seen too much suffering over the past two decades (and before) not to understand themselves as at the receiving end of the policies of an imperial state. The security apparatus is too visible and intrusive on a daily basis to be understood as anything other than a reminder of an occupation force and a subject people. And there has been no justice offered for even the most egregious acts of violence committed by the military, the paramilitary, or the police. There have been spectacular instances of murder, torture, and rape, and no immediate moves to bring criminals to justice, and that has been the case all of this year too, from the killings at Macchil to the unprovoked shooting of boys in Srinagar.

Sunday, August 1: I read about a statement issued by the Central Committee of the CPI (Maoist) offering an "Inquilabi Salaam" to Kashmiris who, in their pursuit, of self-determination, are being crushed by their common enemy, the Indian state. The enemy is the same, they say, in Dandakaranya as in Kashmir. What they self-servingly fail to mention is that their political and military methods are not those of Kashmiris today. And this is an important distinction, and crucial to understanding why the valence of the state "crackdown" is not the same in each theater of conflict. Some Kashmiris have a different comparison for their struggle: their resistance is like the Palestinian Intifada (minus Hamas), and the visual analogy—stone pelters versus armed state forces—is compelling.

And the situation worsens today: eight more are killed, including a young woman, scores wounded, another SOG camp is burned, as is a Tehsildar's office. Villagers who live adjoining the Jammu-Srinagar highway are blockading sections, which invites quick reprisals, since that is the primary road link between India and the valley. The range of protests widens, and it is clear that no official response, however swift, is working. There are ministerial delegations visiting districts in north and south Kashmir, but members of the government have no credibility at all, and their meetings with local officials seem to be exercises in futility. Mehbooba Mufti of the opposition Peoples Democratic Party is refreshingly honest when she says that there is no point in mainstream politicians like her attempting to speak to the people now—they will not listen, she says.

The conversation here shifts increasingly to the imposition of governor's rule, and the handing over of roads and major installations to the army. However, a friend points out that Delhi is able to perform this sort of deployment even when there is an elected government in place, so why would they remove the fig leaf that the elected Chief Minister Omar Abdullah provides? In any case no political activity of any sort is feasible before this cycle of violence—demonstrations and official reprisals—is broken, and no one, least of all the government, seems to know how to enable that. I am reminded of Jayaprakash Narayan's comment on the imposition of the Emergency: "*Vinaash kale vipreet buddhi.*" It is true that in difficult times, when you need them most, the *buddhi*, the mind and the imagination, work least well. In this case, the political imagination has been caused to atrophy, overtaken entirely by the polarized power of the state and the single-minded separatist slogan of "azadi."

I ask a wise friend here what he thinks might happen if tomorrow the Center says that they would talk to the entire range of Kashmiri political opinion without preconditions, that is, without insisting that Kashmir's future necessarily lies within the parameters of the Indian Constitution. I don't know, he says, and in any case these moments of heightened violence are not a good time to begin to think about such future possibilities. Times of peace, or rather, times when daily violence is absent, those are the right moments to initiate political dialogue and action, but those are precisely the moments when governments, lulled into a false sense of security and complacence, do nothing. In any case such inaction suits government, whose actors seem to believe that economic development and employment, thin as they are in practice, will be the magic wands that will wave away political aspirations.

There is no peace, not today. In fact there has been enough violence for the prime minister to call a late-night meeting of the Cabinet Committee on Security. Every one waits to hear what will emerge, and the results are predictable. Omar Abdullah's government is asked to intervene more personally and capably, punishment is promised to all those who take the law into their own hands (that is, all those on the streets who disobey curfew restrictions, and worse, revenge themselves upon those elements of the administration they have come to hate). Abdullah has also appeared on television to make a tepid appeal for calm, but it is too little, too late. His pained face and tone lack conviction.

We hear the sounds of massed people in the first half of the night and occasional shots. But our neighborhood, like so many others in Srinagar where the well-off live, is quiet. Quiet enough to let the sounds of struggle elsewhere waft indistinctly but ominously into our homes.

Monday, August 2: The action on the street shows no let up, and Omar Abdullah is in Delhi for a meeting with the prime minister and others. He emerges and makes an eloquent appeal for peace (the police have been instructed to be restrained, but violence will have consequences, he says) in his English-language press conference after. He repeats his request in

Urdu later in the day for local consumption here. He calls for a calm that will allow the proper education of children and young adults so that they can be competitive in the job market. He also promises the massive recruitment of young people to an unspecified set of jobs—once again, the government offers its payroll as a solution to the problem of political disenchantment. But he does offer a phrase that should be remembered at all times, not just in this moment of crisis: he has told the Center, he says, that Kashmir needs a "political," not just an "economic" package. There are no details offered, but at least there is now a phrase with which to work.

Phrases to work with, a new and respectful semantics—a journalist friend tells me that that is what both the government and Kashmiris need. The government plays strategic games in which the vocabulary they use for the political (not the parliamentary) opposition is charged and designed to belittle: they are the instigators of unrest, they are irrelevant, they are obstacles in the path to development. Small wonder then that Kashmiris see the government as colonial, mainstream politicians as stooges, and the military and paramilitaries as occupation forces. In the absence of a new, more innovative, more polite idiom, there is going to be no way of climbing out of the deep rut in which we find ourselves.

Sadly, eight more people are shot dead, and people have lost track of numbers of the wounded. I keep thinking of the multiplier effects of such violence: for each person dead or injured, there are a score personally affected, and each funeral cortege reminds larger groups of past losses. But then these are the most recent, intense episodes in a longer history of violence. If 70,000 Kashmiris have been killed (regardless of by whom) in the last two decades, then there is virtually no family exempt from the eddying effects of such loss. This is the reservoir of grief, anger, and frustration that produces the flood of emotion that moves people into risking their lives on the street; and sometimes, as we know, floods overwhelm the thickest embankments we build to contain them.

There is also the highly intrusive security footprint to think about. I had travelled in Punjab in the worst years of the Khalistan movement, and I remember just how humiliating and fear-inducing it was to be stopped and questioned over and over again, to have your car searched, and occasionally to be patted down. This is how Kashmiris have lived for twenty years now. No one goes anywhere, even in times of relative peace, without being aware of surveillance and checkpoints. An entire generation—the young on the streets now—have grown up with no other sense of the Indian state. India is the jawan who slaps you because it has been a long day and you are less patient in the checking line than he would like; India is the officer who smiles sardonically as you are pushed to the ground and kicked for good measure; India is the force that tears you and your family from your home to stand around for hours as entire neighborhoods are cordoned off and searched. And this is low-level business. There have been far harsher crimes committed by state agents, but no one has been punished, and that fact alone rankles and will not die.

I speak on the phone to a relative who was a career bureaucrat: utter lawlessness, he says, it needs to be put down firmly, no one should feel entitled to damage property or attack the police. He wonders why things have been allowed to slide in the past few days. I suggest that we have been on this slope for at least twenty years now, and that we have a political rather than a law-and-order problem, but he wants none of that. Various friends and relatives have been calling to ask after us—we don't leave the house and are fine, we say. No we aren't planning to leave. This is home, my mother says, and the weather is lovely.

Tuesday, August 3: A friend with a press pass escorts me past the razor wire that closes off our neighborhood from Maulana Azad Road. We are asked a few questions by the police, which I let him answer, and then we step into the shuttered world of the market. On our route, we pass by a government office protected by CRPF jawans. They are used to seeing my mother walk by—she is the only woman in a sari for miles—and they ask my journalist friend about the day's events. He tells them, and then I say to one of them (miles away from his home in Tamilnadu): this is all terrible, is it not? He nods wanly, and says, *"kya karein, aisa hi ho raha hai"* (what to do, this is what is going on). My mother tells me that these jawans greet her and talk to her each time she walks by them, and that their loneliness is palpable. They are young men, far from home, underpaid, underrested, and occasionally underfed, deployed into a situation in which they know that they are loathed for their uniforms. No shining nationalist zeal or commitment brings them here; their poverty renders them cogs in the machinery of the state, and they well know that.

There are only police on the streets—there is after all a "shoot at sight" order in place—and I smile at the young policeman who has been issued a lathi for offensive action and worn out batsman's pads as defensive equipment. What kind of game do the police authorities think they are playing? What manner of crowd control might be enabled by such equipment? We walk across the market and into the press enclave. Reporters and photographers have been spending nights in their offices, since they are never sure that they will be able to make it to their homes at night or back to their offices the next day.

Five more are dead today (twenty-seven in the last five days), and, worst of all, an eight-year-old boy has been beaten to death. The police issue a statement saying that he died in a stampede of protestors, but there are eyewitnesses who say that he, cricket bat in hand, was raising slogans for azadi and was not quick enough to run away when the CRPF charged. Several jawans beat him, dragged him into their vehicle, and then decided to dump him on the side of the road. He died, not long after, in hospital. Clubbing an eight-year-old boy to death? What kind of harm could he have done, mighty with his cricket bat? Ah yes, perhaps he too picked up and slung stones at the police.

There seems no escaping the impasse here: more dead protestors, more angry protest, more protestors killed. Upon the Chief Minister's request, the Home Ministry has flown in 2,000 paramilitary men, but it is clear to no one what purpose such reinforcements will serve. They are trained no differently from the hundreds of thousands of uniformed men already in service in Kashmir, so how will their presence be a deterrent? They will join the daily rotation, I'm sure, and allow some others overburdened with duties some respite, but it isn't more troops that are needed here, but different forms of policing. Some very senior retired Indian police officers have issued statements saying that police should be instructed never to fire above the waist of protestors, but that advice seems likely to be ignored.

And it isn't only imaginative policing that is missing. People are so stunned by the turn of events and the shocking violence, that nothing seems to emanate from the many civil society organizations at work in Kashmir. Many lack local credibility in any case, but the turn of events here has closed off the possibility of any initiatives or efforts at mediation between people and the state. There is a vast population here holding its collective breath, and I am sure many are wondering, as they have in the past, *after such knowledge, what forgiveness*? And that is what it means to be a Kashmiri in Kashmir today.

....

It is now clear that visible edge of the *tehreek* is no longer *mujahideen* shooting guns, but young boys (and the occasional woman) throwing stones, and they have the support of their families and neighbors. As they are hunted down, their support base widens, and the circles of people who know someone killed or injured or beaten or arrested eddy outwards, till even those who are ambivalent in their support for independence are militant in their alienation from India and its heavy-handed security agents. Hospitals and medical centers can barely cope with the huge influx of the wounded, and there are repeated instances of patients dying before they can get to a hospital because their vehicles, including ambulances, are held up or denied transit at checkpoints.

This sort of turmoil and struggle is a way of life now, the supposed exception that has become the norm. And of course there is an entire generation that has grown up after 1989 that knows the Indian state only in the form of the intrusive actions of the Army or the various paramilitary forces, that is, an entire generation whose politics and sense of self are shaped by their constant interaction with the militarized state, with everyday brutality that can only be experienced as the actions of an occupying power.[2] And everywhere, including among those who work in the government or who cannot see independence in their future, is the awareness that they are being held hostage to an idea of India whose vocabulary and imagination refuse any sense of their historical difference, of their being *Kashmiri* centuries before modern nation-states came into existence. The colonial politics, and the bloodtides, of Partition altered the demography of many districts in the erstwhile princely state of Jammu and Kashmir as Hindus and Muslims made their forced marches away from their localities, and then the events of October 1947 led to the lines of control that are now de facto borders. Six decades later, Kashmiris still organize in the name of an older history and culture that militates against the boundaries drawn for them by India and Pakistan. Neither nation-state, as we know well, has any use for such independence of thought or territory, and the struggle continues.

For someone like me, this struggle is no longer only about indepen-dence for Kashmiris. Over the decades, the Indian response to the *teh-reek* has been so unimaginative and fundamentally coercive that I now believe that Kashmir reveals very forcefully the dangerous fault lines of state functioning in independent India. As armed action becomes more central to the modernizing Indian state's methods of governance (and this is of course true not only in Kashmir), as the mandates of "national de-velopment" are enforced against the desires and the good of local lives and livelihoods, as cultural and historical difference at the margins of the nation (or indeed in its forested heartlands) are abused and denied, the struggle for Kashmir has become a crucial contemporary battleground for the legitimacy, morality, and political vision of postcolonial India. In this way, the Kashmiri struggle for self-determination has, regardless of the future, rendered inescapable a broad re-examination of the definition of India, and more particularly of the unthinking ease with which the state suspends political and civil procedures in order to deal with challenges to its priorities and policies. This is why I am convinced once again, even more so than before, that Indian democracy will live or shrivel poison-ously in Kashmir.

NOTES

1. For a summary and analysis of the Amarnath dispute in 2008, see Tremblay 2009 (esp. pp. 938–945).

2. For a recent instance (July 2013) of the murderous friction between paramilitary forces and the civilian population, this time in the Gool area of Ramban, see Kaul 2013.

Children playing *saz-loung*—hopscotch | Srinagar, February 2007

Children hold up empty cartridges after a police shooting during a protest |
Srinagar, August 2008

"Shahzadah" Rafiq

Ghazal

Vāv vihul tu' nār hāhākār
Lāśi nẙthu' nani mazār hāhākār

Hạnṭh tēśal vunal tu' tshaṭh khōfal
Āvu' su'zmut bahār hāhākār

Yạgi kōtur robūd zọn khūnīn
Thānthriōvmut qarar hāhākār

Teśinyomut sodur malar qạtil
Zāgi rēnzạli mazār hāhākār

Lōl halpath tu' hạnilad havas
Vēlrēvmut amār hāhākār

Kātsh qalmas tu' phōnṭh kākaz davāt
Khūnu' ghọtu' dith chi śār hāhākār

"Shahzadah" Rafiq

Ghazal

Wild winds and fire, an uproar afoot
Bodies—naked—a grave, an uproar afoot

Barren, angry fog and the fearsome cold wind
Comes a sodden spring, an uproar afoot

Wood pigeons turned numb, thoughts bloodied
Peace of mind, trembling and shivering, an uproar afoot

The sea turned furious, waves murderous
The angel of death stalks—a grave—an uproar afoot

Love goes mad and desire is blamed
Longing is entrapped, an uproar afoot

Weakened pen, and shrunken paper-ink
Couplets dipped in blood, an uproar afoot

....

Published in *Sheeraza* (Kashmiri) 27:5 (1993), 102.

"Shahzadah" Rafiq is the pen name of Mohammed Rafiq Gawaie, who was born in 1957 in Meemander Shopian. He received his BA from Government Degree College, Anantnag. He began writing poetry while young, and also writes critical essays on literary topics. He publishes a journal on culture titled *Saqafat*.

Bashir Dada

du'āyikhạr karus pot ālav dis

du'āyikhạr karus pot ālav dis yā oś dadu'rāy trāv matiō
yus śām ḍạlith az nanu'vōruy garu' trạ̄vith kuhas kot drāv matiō

yinu' yād me pāvakh zū nērы̆m chum kūt paḍāvas tāni pakun
thaku'ros paku' tiūtah yūt vanakh poz mīlu' kanē nạhnāv matiō

cham ṭạ̄ṭh me, ạśku'ni nākạ̄mī zạ̄nith mạnith nākām gatshav
ba ti śām bạnith thepi thepi tshānḍath tsu' ti ban subaḥ tạy rāv matiō

chus kafan vạlith poz āś cham tsu'ti āsakh mātam dāran manz
dы̆v marnu' patay voṇi hōl tsalы̆m volu' pānay me metsital sāv matiō

beyi dilu'kы̆n zakhman krōl vothы̆m maẓlūm panun dil rachnu' moẖhay
lari lạzim cạnis nāvas chuy maẓlūm Bạṣīrun nāv matiō

Bashir Dada

Bless Him Now

Bless him now, call out to him, let flow streams of tears, o lost one[1]
He, who in evening's dark, left home—bare-foot—for the mountains,
o lost one

Do not remind me, for my life will ebb, of the distance I have to walk
to my rest
I'll walk without tiring, as far as you say—only smash the milestones,
o lost one

For I cherish the failures of love—and willingly we will fail:
I—become the evening—will search for you everywhere; as you—
become the morning—disappear, o lost one

I wear a shroud, and hope in truth that you too will be among my
mourners—
Death might fulfill my desires, and you will lay me to sleep, under earth,
o lost one

The scabs on my heart's wounds have ripped again: to salve my oppressed
heart—
Alongside your name—it is necessary—write oppressed *Bashir*,
o lost one.[2]

....

Original in Kashmiri, Published in *Naghma te Beath* (*Musical Songs*), compiled and
edited by Dr Afaq Aziz (Srinagar: Writers Organization for Research and Development,
2003), 106.

Bashir Dada was born in 1952 in Anantnag. He is a professional actor and also has
produced programs for Doordarshan Kashmir. His literary works include *Hum Chinaar
Walein Hain, Paanch Draamay*, and *Zorum ne Doorer*. He has won awards (including the
Akashvani Annual Award) for both his acting and his writing.

1. The phrase "o lost one" translates the Kashmir word *matyov*, which can mean lunatic, but also someone possessed by an ideal or spirit that supersedes rationality (the same word is used, with powerful effect, by Mohiuddin 'Massarat' in his "Ghazal").

2. A version of this lyric has been sung by Waheed Jilani and the video can be viewed at http://www.youtube.com/watch?v=SuPTSbWBv2U, accessed on May 19, 2014.

Abandoned Kashmiri Pandit homes | Haal Shopian, October 2012

Naji Munawar

Teli tu'az

"Tshạvrāv gāś"
    "Bihith kath pȳṭh chukh?"

"Dah ziādu' āsan bajēmu'ts"

    "Teli hē rạti rātas ōs gāś vuzvun āsān!
Dazvunuy āsān!"

"Voni kath pȳṭh chakh vōlān?"
"Vāhi teli ạsi dapān anigoṭ mā nȳnglāvi
Tu' voni chu gāś pazī khȳni yivān."

Naji Munawar

Then and Today

"Put out the light"

    "What are you sitting on?"

"It must be past ten o'clock"

    "Then oh! all night the light kept burning.
Kept on burning."

"Now what are you getting enraged about?"

"Alas, then it used to be said that the darkness might swallow—
and now the light truly comes to devour."

....

Published in *Sheeraza* (Kashmiri) 31:4 (1996), 83.

Naji Munawar was born in 1934 in Kaprin (Shopian). He writes poetry, literary history, and children's literature, and has discovered and compiled the work of nineteenth-century Kashmiri poets. He has also translated Sophocles and Shakespeare into Kashmiri. His volume of criticism, *Pursaan*, won the Sahitya Akademi award in 2002.

Rukhsana Jabeen

Nazm

Yu' mōt kōtāh bē ār

Kū'tẏn śurẏn yatīm tshu'nān
Tu' mājan poṭhu'r nivān nu' khōtsān
Benẏn yu' kū'tsan nivān baẏ
Bē vāy pāṭhẏn garay vujārān

Kaman javānan yu' mōt paninyn pakhan andar nith
Mazāri mēts tal hamēś bāpath nindu'r chu pāvān

Śōngith chu yēthi mētsi andar
Su rāyil javān tu'
Yem su'nd irādu' thaḍi ās

Safēd tsādar valith az amis
Tu' khāb voni zan maśith gamit tas
Tamām hasrat tu' ārzō yeti tsẏnin tu' dūr piav

Dohas vanān doh tu' kālu'obras su kālu'obraẏ vanān rōziōv

Sẏṭhāh pariōhas zi
Rāts pahran tsa van duhul

Poz
Su poz vanān gō

Rukhsana Jabeen

Nazm

This Death, how pitiless

How many children it renders orphans
And, without fear, takes sons from mothers
From so many sisters it takes brothers
Without sympathy it devastates homes

Such youths this death takes under its wings
Beneath graveyard-earth forever puts them to sleep

Sleeping in this soil
Is that valorous young one too
Whose ambitions were high

A white shroud wraps around him today
And dreams are now as if forgotten by him
All desires and wishes left here, and he now distant

The day he named the day, called dark clouds, dark clouds, kept calling

He was tutored at length to
Call the hours of the night the day

Truth
Speaking the truth he went

....

Published in *Sheeraza* (Kashmiri) 31:4 (1997), 70–71.

Rukhsana Jabeen was born in 1955 in Srinagar. She has an MA in Urdu and an MA
and M.Phil. in Persian. She is currently station director, Radio Kashmir. Her collection
of Urdu poems, *Chiragh Chehra*, is under publication. She is currently translating Hafiz
Shirazi's Persian verse into Kashmiri.

Arshad Mushtaq

Teli lāyi me kani

Yeli lōlas me kạṇḍitār gạndu'kh
Teli lāyi me kani

Yeli khāb miōn mismār korukh
Teli lāyi me kani

Yeli gōli calāvŷkh śīr khwāras;
Me khūnas lạj grŷkh
Yeli mạnzi mahrāz kabri borukh
Teli lāyi me kani

Yeli gạrīb mọṇḍi hund garu' zōlukh
Jai Hind vanān
Yeli yeli ẓulmas dastār goṇḍukh
Teli lāyi me kani

Yeli Lal Dŷd trạvu'kh vuriyān yimav
Rambiār baṭhī
Yeli Zūni ạchan tal mōrukh Yūsuf
Teli lāyi me kani

Yeli Vŷthi manz rōtli trōvukh
Satan benŷn hund bōy
Yeli mōtu' nindri
Aku' nandun sōvukh
Teli lāyi me kani

Arshad Mushtaq

That's When I Threw Stones

When they tied barbed wire to my love
That's when I threw stones!

When they shattered my dream
That's when I threw stones.

When they fired at a suckling baby
My blood rose to a boil,
When they stuffed in a grave a hennaed groom
That's when I threw stones!

When they torched a poor widow's home
Saying "Jai Hind,"
Each time they honored oppression
That's when I threw stones!

When they left Lal Dĕd naked
On the bank of the Rambiar,[1]
When they killed Yousuf before Zooni's eyes[2]
That's when I threw stones!

When in darkness into the Vyeth they threw
A brother of seven sisters,
When into death's sleep
They lulled Akanandun,[3]
That's when I threw stones.

....

This poem (published on September 12, 2010) is available in a Roman transcription at www.facebook.com/notes/aarsh-mushtaq/telle-laaye-mea-kainna-kashmiri-poem-by -aarsh-m/161056957241422.

Arshad Mushtaq was born in 1972 in Srinagar. He received his BA in English from Sri Venkateswara College, Delhi University and an MA in journalism and mass communication from University of Kashmir. In 2011, he was an International Fellow at the Documentary Center, George Washington University. He writes plays and directs theatre and film.

NOTES

1. Lal Děd, the fourteenth-century mystic poet whose verses are part of the fabric of Kashmiri, is said to have (in the manner of some otherworldly ascetics) wandered naked. Here her nakedness refers to the murder of Neelofar Jan (twenty-two) and her sister-in-law Aasiya Jan (seventeen), whose bodies were found on May 30, 2009 in the Rambiar River at Shopian. The mysterious circumstances of their deaths and the public suspicion that they had been raped and killed by security men led to widespread protests, curfews, and police action in which more people were killed and injured.

2. Zooni was the childhood name of Habba Khatoon, the sixteenth-century mystic poet, who married the ruler of Kashmir, Yusuf Shah Chak. The invading army of the Mughal Emperor Akbar deposed and exiled Yusuf Shah Chak to Bihar, where he died and is buried.

3. Akanandun is an enormously popular Kashmiri folktale that tells of a yogi's boon that grants a baby boy to a king and queen who have seven daughters. The yogi however stipulates that he will return for the boy in twelve years. Not only does he do so, but he insists that Akanandun be sacrificed and cooked for his meal. The boy's parents are forced to comply, but their misery is turned to joy once it turns out that the yogi's powers have in fact kept Akanandun alive, and that this ordeal was only the yogi's method of testing their promise! Like some other folktales, "Akanandun" features egregious violence before it arrives at its hopeful resolution—in this poem, however, we know only Akanandun's death, not his revival.

A Kashmiri Pandit woman looks out from a window of her home | Haal Shopian, October 2012

Ayesha "Mastoor"

su chu śur

Su chu śur
Tas cha nu' khabar kenh
Tas chu nu' me varạy kānh

Poṭru' dạdis vŷtrih nūn
Vāhi oś tu' batu' khion

Lạś gạṇḍnas
Tu' mujādlas drāv
Jạphi lạji

Pōśi ṭūri putsnin
Trēśi hạti pạvin

Hōlu' dor tu' lōlu' hot dapan
"Lạginas nārā
Gạtshinas talukh pŷṭh
Vạthinas alu'gạbu' traṭu' buznāh
Yuth nu' kạynātas rōzī kānh"

    .....

Su chu śur
Śuri gindnā karān
Ḥad chu pozuy
Band mā vāti karun
qạdu' band gav azāb sakh
poṭru' dạdis lalu'vu'nī sŷkh
kus tu' kas
pāk Maryamun[A.S.]
Nēk ḥaz 'Īsā[A.S.]
Dāras khōrukh

Ayesha "Mastoor"

He Is but a Child

He is but a child
He knows nothing
He has no one but me

The pain of losing a child is as salt on wounds
Oh! to eat tears-and-rice

An ardor possessed him
And he went for battle
The fight began

The buds of flowers, shredded
The already parched, defeated

Aching with pain and miserable with love, she will say
"Let it catch fire
May all turn upside-down
May lightning sear unexpectedly
Let no one remain in the universe"

    .....

He is but a child
At child's play
Limits are fair
But we can't shut him up
Being locked up is great suffering
The pain of losing a child is as cradling sand
Who and whom

Virgin Mary's[A.S.]
The good Hazrat Jesus[A.S.]
Raised to the crucifix

Kuni ạch hund gāś
Path kun rūdmut
mọnḍu'h kārvānas
Brōnh kani tshạyvruk

"Yāras mā gav kānh gum vār"

Suchu śur
Śuri gindnā karān
Tas cha nu' khabar kenh
Tas chu nu' me varạy kānh

The light of my eye[1]
Left behind
Snuffed in front
Of the caravan of widows

"The careless lover did not even break a sweat"

He is but a child
At child's play
He knows nothing
He has no one but me

....

Published in *Sheeraza* (Kashmiri) 27:5 (1993), 104–05.

Ayesha 'Mastoor' was born in 1935 in Srinagar. She received an MA in Urdu and taught in government institutions, retiring as professor of Urdu at Government Women's College, Nawa Kadal, Srinagar. Her first collection of poetry was published in 2006. She was a well-known poet, but most of her work is yet to be compiled.

NOTE

1. "The light of my eye" refers idiomatically to her only son.

Maqbool "Sajid"

Ghazal

Vujāru' gạy śahar śahar vọn rūd kẙā
Banēy yi zindgī qahar vọn rūd kẙā

Vuchith yikun raśik jahān karān ōs
Su bāgh az chu akh khanḍar vọn rūd kẙā

Tsọpạ̄ri mōtạ̄s yeti vạhu'ri vạhu'ri
Hutẙn qabar yetẙn qabar vọn rūd kẙā

Gatshān gul tsọpạ̄ri hardu' vāvu' buzi
Vadān chi yeti achar achar vọn rūd kẙā

Chu prẙth akhā vọn jāyi jāyi dam bakhọd
Chu mā sa kānh ti bekhatar vọn rūd kẙā

Vatan ḍọlān cha jāyi jāyi lāśu' hā
Garu' ki garay pemu'ti pathar vọn rūd kẙā

Maqbool "Sajid"

Ghazal

Cities upon cities have become desolate, now what is left
This life has become oppressive, now what is left

Looking towards here, the world was envious
That garden today is a ruin, now what is left

In every direction here death's mouth opens wide
There a grave, here a grave, now what is left

Flowers in every direction burn in the autumn wind
Word upon word weeps here, now what is left

Everyone is now speechless in place upon place
Is there any one not in danger, now what is left

Corpses are strewn unattended upon paths, in place upon place
Homes upon homes have fallen down, now what is left

....

Published in *Sheeraza* (Kashmiri) 31:4 (1997), 136.

Maqbool 'Sajid' was born in 1969 in Khushpora, Srinagar. He graduated from Amar Singh College, took an MA in Kashmiri from Kashmir University, and wrote an M.Phil. thesis on "Old Values and New Trends in Modern Kashmiri Literary Criticism." He publishes both literary criticism and poetry.

Women scuffle with police during a gun battle between militants and government forces | Arwani Kulgam, January 2013

Devotees seek blessings at the Hazratbal shrine | Srinagar, February 2012

"My Paradise Is Burnin' . . ."

Past and Present in the Challenge of Kashmir

THE SITUATION TODAY

The bloody disruption of civic and political order in Kashmir and the massive Indian security apparatus has meant that for long stretches of time in the last two decades, large sections of the state have been turned into armed camps. The military, paramilitary, and police forces have been very successful in apprehending or killing militants, but along with every militant eliminated, scores of other Kashmiris have been picked up, tortured, or imprisoned on suspicion of being affiliated with some form of profreedom activism. Worse, there are large numbers of those who simply disappeared, and whose unidentified bodies now lie in unmarked graves, some of which have been investigated by human rights groups in the last few years (International People's Tribunal 2009). Conflicts between different factions of the *tehreekis* also led to large-scale internecine killings. The government played a role here too, encouraging "surrendered" militants to turn their arms against each other, and enrolling them into loosely regulated, much-feared ancillaries of the uniformed police force (Human Rights Watch 1996; the recent trove of diplomatic cables released by Wikileaks provides unusual corroboration—see the *Guardian* report on December 16, 2010, "US Embassy Cables: US Argues against Visa for Kashmiri 'Paramilitary'"). The numbers of the dead have mounted; the numbers of those maimed physically and psychologically are even larger.

I offer this bare-bones summary here to make a simple point: there exists no Kashmiri family that has not suffered from the war raging around them. There are material reminders of their suffering everywhere: thousands of gravestones now sprout in fresh graveyards all over Srinagar and other towns in Kashmir, and their inscriptions bear witness to martyrs who have sacrificed themselves in the cause of independence. Hospitals and dispensaries report astonishing numbers of people afflicted with mental illnesses (Wax 2008). In times of conflict, including during the new *intifada* of summer 2010,[1] these hospitals were barely able to cope with the influx of the dying and the damaged. Local newspapers, magazines, and the electronic media are full of reports of human misery. Various "fact-finding missions" originating in India, and some international human rights organizations, have long documented the military and civil abuses that accompany "crackdowns" (this is the word used locally) on civilian populations. Details of these abuses are not hidden, even if the crisis itself, in spite of media attention in recent years, has not become a definitive political problem for contemporary India or indeed for the international community. A generation and more have come of age in Kashmir knowing only the brutality and the everyday suspicions of a civic order riddled with informers for the state or for antistate groups, and for many of them, it remains incomprehensible why a nation lauded as the world's largest democracy has remained immune to their suffering.

COLONIAL HISTORY, POSTCOLONIAL GOVERNANCE

Much of the violence that has transpired in Kashmir is familiar from other contexts across the globe. It is noteworthy here because it plays out crucial contradictions of the modern democratic, putatively *postcolonial*, state. After all, the founding rationale for postcolonial and democratic nation-states is the consent of the different subnational communities in whose name anticolonial movements demanded and gained independence. Further, postcolonial democracies are meant to enable more equitable and indeed sustainable forms of development, especially those that will encourage the restructuring of historical socioeconomic and cultural hierarchies intensified or precipitated by colonial rule.

In practice, as we know, most once-colonized nations (including those that are electoral democracies) continue to reinforce many of the socioeconomic arrangements and administrative and policing functions bequeathed to them by the colonial state (as I argue in the last chapter of this volume). This history partly explains the increasingly centripetal and rigid form of nationalism that came to dominate the political cultures of newly independent nations, and it is certainly crucial to understanding the relationship of the Indian state with Kashmir. Postcolonial nations did not of course invent this form of militarized patriotism; over the course of the nineteenth century, imperial nations put on display its ritual, administrative, and civic forms in their colonies, and celebrated it as the ethical core of modern citizenship.

The formation of colonial "nations" (if territories brought under foreign rule could be called that) also emphasized this sort of centralized military power. As colonial rulers cobbled together territories through conquest and alliance, they reshaped the forms of political collectivity that had defined these territories. Smaller territorial entities ruled by kings, their feudatories, even large landowners, with poorly defined, porous, and shifting borders between them were yoked together under a common authority. In many cases, it was the practical limits of colonial authority that demarcated what were to become the borders of new nations. Thus, when anticolonial movements demanded the right to self-determination and political governance, they spoke for a "nation" that was often the product of a comparatively recent colonial history, and that contained disparate communities historically unequal in their relations with each other, but now tenuously united in their opposition to colonial rule. In British India, for instance, several communities at the extremities of India and Pakistan found themselves, for various reasons, incorporated into these new nations.

At its greatest extent, the British Empire in South Asia ranged from its northwestern reaches in what is now Afghanistan to its southern tip in Ceylon (today's Sri Lanka) to its eastern territories in Burma (now Myanmar). Large sections of these lands were not ruled directly by the British. There existed many kingdoms nominally under the control of local maharajas and nawabs, even though all of them were bound in treaty relations with, and existed as vassals of, the British monarch, and several had British residents supervising their political, military, and civic administration. Such was the case with the state of Jammu and Kashmir. The modern contours of the kingdom were put into place by the Sikh Maharaja Ranjit Singh of Lahore, whose forces took large territories in Jammu and the valley of Kashmir in 1819, spoils of their successful campaigns against the Afghan Durrani rulers. Three years later, he confirmed one of his highly successful

Dogra generals, Gulab Singh Jamwal, as raja of Jammu. By 1840, Gulab Singh's armies extended the kingdom into Ladakh and Baltistan. In 1846, after the British East India Company, victors of the First Anglo-Sikh war, gained control of Punjab, they signed treaties confirming Gulab Singh as the maharaja of Jammu and Kashmir, a state they saw as a buffer between them and the Afghans, Russians, and Chinese. For the British, Jammu and Kashmir was central to their forward-areas policies in the northwest of India, whose mountain ranges, valleys, and high-altitude passes they thought critical to their defence against Russian expansion, or even Chinese control of trade routes in Tibet and Ladakh. Thus, between 1888 and 1892, the state's territories were extended into Gilgit, Hunza, and Nagar by troops commanded by British officers acting ostensibly on behalf of Kashmir's ruler, Ranbir Singh (Gulab Singh's son).

This brief outline of the extension of Dogra rule and British authority suggests more clarity of command and control than was the case in these often-contested territories and their fought-over and poorly demarcated boundaries (for an overview, written largely from the points of view available in British imperial archives, see Huttenback 2004). As a matter of imperial policy, the British had allowed princely states throughout India their formal apparatus of independent governance and revenue collection, while making sure that they maintained British trading, military, and diplomatic priorities. This process often involved considerable give-and-take between the British and the local ruler, whether it involved raising troops, waging war, or setting up revenue, judicial, and educational institutions within the state. Jammu and Kashmir was no different, with the proviso that its strategic location meant that, in the second half of the nineteenth century, the British were primarily concerned with fixing and strengthening the state's northwestern borders. If they intervened in the internal affairs of the state, they did so largely because they believed misrule, particularly excessive taxation, would produce social instability that would weaken the state's authority in its border areas (Rai 2004:142–44).

The most consequential feature of the state of Jammu and Kashmir was the fact that its Dogra Hindu maharajas ruled over a majority Muslim population. This was not in itself unique amongst princely states in India, where there are many instances of "minority" rulers developing policies that did not differentiate egregiously between their subjects in favor of their coreligionists. However, as Mridu Rai has demonstrated persuasively, the Dogra rulers' policies so derived from their identity as Rajput Hindus and so resolutely catered to their Hindu affiliations, within the state and outside it, that the Dogra state became, in effect, a Hindu state (Rai 2004: 7). The vast majority of Muslim peasants and indeed city-based artisans saw none of the benefits of centralized administration; they continued to live at subsistence levels while being forced to yield both unpaid labor (*begar*) virtually on demand, as well as crippling taxes on their produce. This was not the case with Kashmiri Hindus (known as Pandits); no more than 5 percent of the population, they wielded disproportionate power as revenue-gatherers, accountants, civic administrators, and landholders. Pandits had developed levels of literacy that made them indispensable to the lower rungs of the administration (particularly given historically abysmal levels of formal learning among Muslims), and this fact, combined with the Dogra emphasis on Hindu affiliates, meant that many Pandits functioned visibly as extensions of the maharaja's power. It is another matter that the Dogras excluded Pandit elites from the higher administration in favor of Dogras or bureaucrats recruited from Punjab and elsewhere; particularly for the large mass of Muslim peasants, Pandits were the Kashmiri-speaking face of state power (Zutshi 2004: 52).

Both Mridu Rai's *Hindu Rulers, Muslim Subjects* and Chitralekha Zutshi's *Languages of Belonging*—books essential to understanding the contemporary crisis in Kashmir—make clear to us the sociology and political force of these social and communitarian divides, as well as their lingering effects into the present. Zutshi develops a careful argument about the growth of political consciousness among Muslims in the last two decades of the nineteenth century and the first two of the twentieth: such political mobilization, even when centered around Islamic community, was, not surprisingly, an internally contested process, as leaders of different groupings derived their priorities from particular regional, sectarian, and socioeconomic affiliations. However, the communitarian "ritual and legal framework" within which all such mobilization was permitted was defined by the Dogra state, and occasionally by British administrators (Zutshi 2004: 118–121). Zutshi also points out that an important concern of newly politicized Muslim elites, particularly those educated outside Kashmir, was the educational backwardness of the community. Their focus on education had a particular end in view: the creation of teachers or bureaucrats in the administration in order to counteract the state's systematic exclusion of

Muslims. Inevitably, the rise of educated Muslims seeking employment in these services led to tensions between them and the Pandits who had long presumed on such positions. It was also the case that since Urdu was the official language of the state, no one argued for instruction in Kashmiri, which meant that illiteracy remained an enormous problem, especially in agricultural areas, perpetuating divides between urban Muslim elites and the rural poor in whose name they claimed to speak (Zutshi 2004: 169–209).

In the 1930s and 1940s, political movements in the state veered between communitarian, regionalist, or pan-nationalist emphases. At different moments, political leaders spoke of a Kashmiri collectivity, ostensibly contained within the boundaries of the princely state, so distinct from political identities elsewhere that it called for its own process of self-determination. At other times they saw themselves as participants in larger nationalist movements, led by the Indian National Congress or the Muslim League, for independence from British rule. As an example, Zutshi tracks shifts in the positions taken by Sheikh Abdullah's All Jammu and Kashmir National Conference, arguably the most important and mass-based political party in Kashmir, which changed its profile considerably over the course of two decades. During this period, political demands made of the Dogra state for Muslim representation in administration developed (in tandem with anticolonial political mobilization in India) into a movement against Dogra rule and for representative government. By the mid-1940s there was a great deal of debate in Kashmir about the pros and cons of allying local movements against the Dogra state with anticolonial movements in British India. Further, there were available full-blown critiques of the National Conference's policies, developed both by those who argued that Kashmiris should pursue their own political ends and by those who insisted that Kashmir's future lay with the Pakistan that Muhammad Ali Jinnah's All-India Muslim League was bringing into being (Zutshi 2004: 227–322).

The give-and-take of politics within and without the state was also shaped by British policies vis-à-vis the Princely States (formally enunciated in the Indian Independence Act of 1947), which allowed the possibility that a state like Jammu and Kashmir would not amalgamate with either India or Pakistan once those nations came into being. Such constitutional open-endedness has caused Alastair Lamb, a historian of the raj, to write that in "one sense the Kashmir problem can be seen as a consequence of the British failure to find a satisfactory method for the integration of the Princely States into the independent India and Pakistan that succeeded the British Raj" (Lamb 1966: 3). By 1947, even though the strength of people's movements for representative government was clear, as were the ties between Jawaharlal Nehru's Indian National Conference and Sheikh Abdullah's J&K National Conference, the then maharaja, the feckless Hari Singh, hoped to retain his position as the ruler of an independent nation even after the British withdrew as the paramount power in India.[2] Jinnah had in turn visited Kashmir in 1944 and had greatly strengthened ties with the (now revived) Kashmiri Muslim Conference, which allowed this organization to represent an alternative future for Kashmir as part of Pakistan. It was also the case that even as Sheikh Abdullah and Nehru considered themselves allies, there had been no substantial discussion (at least not any that was public knowledge) about Kashmir's future after August 15, 1947. British rule was to end, but there were no certainties about the maharaja's rule in Kashmir, against which the National Conference and other Kashmiri political parties continued to campaign, even though many of their leaders were in jail.

As both Rai and Zutshi make clear, political activity in Jammu and Kashmir had long been driven by connections established between people within the state and their compatriots elsewhere in British India, even though some Kashmiri nationalists argued that they needed to address problems of governance within the state rather than getting caught up in the larger anticolonial movement. This isolationism was even then an untenable idea, as borders, no matter how heavily policed, cannot prevent the transmission of political ideas and policies, and in particular cannot guard against the urgency of momentous current events as they hurtled along at this moment of supercharged social turmoil. For the idea of Partition, as we know well, brought along with it the possibility of unprecedented dislocations of populations, as millions of Muslims prepared to move to Pakistan and an equal number of Hindus and Sikhs to India. In fact, these massive relocations were far more frantic and haphazard when they took place, and that frenzy was directly caused by communal attacks, massacres, and riots in different parts of India in the run-up to independence, as well as just after. A great deal of recent scholarly work has clarified for us the mix of motivated violence (that is, violence arranged by individuals or groups designed to gain land, property, or goods by driving out particular communities) and fearful uncertainty that precipitated these massive population shifts. Most immediately, such violence seemed to demonstrate, even legitimize by dramatizing spectacularly, the unbridgeable divides between Hindus and Muslims insisted upon by ideologues of communal difference (Brass 2003; Pandey 2001).

. . . .

PARTITION LEGACIES

The forced movement of populations, as well as the religious polarization confirmed by Partition violence, are of great consequence to the history of the last half-century in Jammu and Kashmir. In fact it is impossible to separate all that happened in 1947 in Jammu Province, particularly in Poonch, from the larger mayhem in Punjab, to which of course Jammu was very well connected. Victoria Schofield is the most recent of commentators on the Kashmir conflict to remind us that, in March 1947, an anti-maharajah "no-tax" campaign (tantamount to a revolt) had begun in Poonch. There were particular reasons for this: Muslims from Poonch and Mirpur had supplied most of the state citizens who had fought in the British Indian Army in World War II (and some had fought against the British in the Indian National Army); when they were demobilized, the maharaja refused to enlist them in his army, and they returned to an oppressive taxation regime enforced by Dogra troops. Further, as communal disturbances broke out in Punjab, and spilled over into Jammu, the maharaja ordered the disarming of Muslims, particularly of those who possessed weapons from their military service, and some of these guns were used to arm Sikhs and Hindus. Already disaffected from the maharajah, Poonchis became the fighting arm of the pro-Pakistan sentiment in the state, and were then mobilized accordingly by Pakistanis (Khan 1970). Schofield, like Alastair Lamb, believes that in order to raise men and armaments, Poonchis contacted tribal affiliates in the Northwestern Areas, and this link became one of the reasons why, in October 1947, tribesmen from these areas crossed the border into Kashmir in support of their beleaguered coreligionists (Schofield 2010: 41–47; Lamb 1966: 37–38).

In addition, after the riots in Rawalpindi and elsewhere in March 1947, large numbers of Hindu and Sikh refugees from western Punjab were forced into the Jammu area, and their presence, and the stories of the horrors they had faced, exacerbated communal divides in the city. By October, as elsewhere in Punjab, sporadic acts of retributive violence had multiplied. In Jammu, a combination of orchestrated violence (eye-witnesses say members of the police and Dogra forces attacked Muslim localities and refugee convoys) and generalized fear caused a huge demographic shift in Jammu city and the *tehsils* to its west (Snedden 2001; Saraf 2004: 161–97; Symonds 2001: 68). Estimates suggest that half a million Muslims were displaced, and 200,000 were killed or died, as refugees, of epidemics and exposure (Stephens 1953: 138, 112; Hasan 2005; Chattha 2011).[3] Members of these displaced groups went on to play important roles in the politics of the territory that Pakistan calls Azad Kashmir, or in Indian terms, Pakistan Occupied Kashmir. Memories of their dispossession and dislocation are often invoked by Pakistani and insurgent groups seeking freedom for Kashmir today.[4]

In effect, the city of Jammu became largely Hindu, and, in a pattern of resettlement that marked Partition events, refugees from Pakistan were resettled into properties that once belonged to Muslims (for a study of parallel resettlement practices in Delhi and Karachi, see Zamindar 2007). In a 2009 interview, Ved Bhasin, the longtime editor of the *Kashmir Times*, described these riots as a deliberate attempt to change the demographics of the plains areas of the state and thus to influence its future ("Riots Changed J&K Politics" 2011). As Yasmin Khan, another recent commentator on Partition puts it, "the mass killing in Jammu and Kashmir in 1947–48, which is usually forgotten or incorporated into the history of Kashmiri wars, shared far more characteristics with other Partition slaughters" (such as those population-clearing exercises orchestrated in the princely states of Bharatpur and Alwar) (Khan 2007: 135; for Bharatpur and Alwar, see Copland 1998 and Mayaram 1997).

For ten weeks after India and Pakistan came into being, the maharaja of Kashmir maintained a tenuous hold on power and the hope that he would rule an independent state. It was clear that if he had to choose, even a majority Muslim population and contiguous borders would not convince him to accede to Pakistan (he was too much the Hindu partisan). As it turned out, the issue was forced for him by the incursion into Kashmir of an estimated five thousand armed tribesmen from northwestern Pakistan (with some support from the Pakistani army and retired soldiers, as well as fighters from Poonch and Mirpur). By October 24, 1947, they had taken several towns en route to Srinagar, which caused Maharaja Hari Singh to request Indian military help, and then, two days later, to sign an Instrument of Accession that legitimized the landing of Indian troops in Srinagar Airport on October 27. (The sequence, and hence the legal validity, of these events is disputed; for the debate, see Schofield 2010: 52–60 and Jha 1998.) For the next fourteen months, the Indian Army battled regular units of the Pakistani army and local militias and irregulars in a number of theaters in Jammu, Kashmir, and Ladakh. On January 1, 1949, a ceasefire under the auspices of the United Nations was declared between Pakistan and India, and the forward positions of each army became, over time (and via other battles in 1965 and 1971), the lines of control between the two nations and thus the boundary between India and Pakistan in this state. But even more consequentially, such prolonged military activities meant that what might have once been a constitutional question of accession became part of the long-drawn out (and ongoing) drama of the Partition of British India, and thus one sequence in the unseemly pageant of violent nation-formation across the subcontinent. As Vazira Zamindar argues, the history of early postcolonial state-formation in India and Pakistan revolved around managing and shaping the "colossal displacements of Partition." In her words, the "highly surveillanced western Indo-Pak border, one of the most difficult for citizens of the region to cross to this day, was not a consequence of the Kashmir conflict, as security studies gurus may suggest, but rather was formed through a series of attempts to resolve the fundamental uncertainty of the political Partition itself" (Zamindar 2007: 3).

This history is of great and continuing importance in understanding the Kashmir conflict in India and in Pakistan, as the divides between Hindus and Muslims that were confirmed in Partition and its attendant violence continue to frame all perceptions of the genesis, and any ideas about the potential solution of the problem. As it is, the former princely state has been divided ever since 1948, with Pakistan controlling Baltistan and Gilgit, the vast swathe of mountains and valleys in the northwest as well as Azad ("Free") Kashmir, a narrow strip of territory to the west of the populous areas of Jammu and Kashmir, which are under Indian control. India also controls Ladakh, while China holds the Aksai Chin plateau in the northeast. For Indian nationalists, the secular credentials of the Indian state are visible in Kashmir's membership of the union, given that it was and is a Muslim majority state, and thus a rebuttal of the "two-nation" theory that birthed Pakistan as the putative homeland of the subcontinent's Muslims. For Pakistani nationalists, Kashmir, precisely because it was and is a Muslim majority state, and because it shares contiguous borders and land routes with Pakistan, was stolen from them by the Dogra Hindu maharaja aided by India's armed forces. For them, this is a land and a people held only by the force of the massive Indian military deployment at the borders and within the state.

The Indian claim was complicated by the fact that the Instrument of Accession itself contained clauses that suggested that the maharaja was not signing away his sovereignty (Clause 8) nor agreeing to function within "any future constitution of India" (Clause 2). Thus, in various forums, both in India and at the United Nations, Jawaharlal Nehru and officials of the Indian government reiterated their belief that this accession had to be ratified by the population at large. It is a moot point whether India was ever going to stage the plebiscite it promised. In any case, the prolonged warfare at the borders of the state, and the need to resettle Partition refugees as well as those created by the fighting, meant that the plebiscite was indefinitely set aside. Internally too, Sheikh Abdullah's popularity meant that the National Conference and its pro-India stand prevailed, and he strengthened his hold by arresting or exiling consequential politicians of a pro-Pakistan bent. He did not however give up his bargaining chip with India, which was the idea of an independent Kashmir. As a result of the military, and then the political give-and-take of the years after 1947, when the Indian constitution was drafted, it included an Article 370, which recognized and guaranteed the special circumstances of Kashmir's accession, and thus its difference from the other states in the Union. All political and administrative processes in the state, including elections to a Constituent Assembly, were to derive their form and function from this arrangement, which was, as subsequent events were to show, flawed in conception and unsustainable in practice.

Most Indian politicians, even those who respected Kashmir's "special status," presumed it was only a question of time before the state would become so economically and socially integrated with India that the provisions of Article 370 would be rendered obsolete in practice. Other national political parties like the Jan Sangh and their allies in the state, the

Praja Parishad, mobilized to try and abrogate Article 370, and made the incorporation of Kashmir into India an important feature of their political agenda. In any case, even in the early 1950s, as part of their attempts to contest the internal hegemony of Kashmiri politicians based in Srinagar, an India-identified set of Hindu political leaders from Jammu, and Buddhist leaders in Ladakh, argued for formal integration within the larger nation. Their efforts did not end in success, but they were reminders that Jammu and Kashmir was by no means a state unitary in its populations or its political aspirations, which remains the case today. Over the next three decades, politics in Jammu and Kashmir continued to be a powder keg of repression (in 1953, Sheikh Abdullah was arrested by the central government and detained, on and off, for two decades after; other politicians suffered similar fates). Election after election was rigged to keep out pro-Pakistani candidates. Relations between the state and a central government were often strained, as the latter repeatedly intervened in local politics and administration. However, while large sections of the rural, and particularly the mountainous, areas of Jammu, Kashmir, and Ladakh remained poor, central investments in development and infrastructure created visible reminders of the benefits of affiliation with India. Ironically, much of this infrastructure, particularly in the border areas, derived directly from India's military priorities, since war against Pakistan in 1965 and 1971 meant a huge build-up of soldiers and armaments in some of the highest and most inhospitable locations in the world. The Indian government could claim to budget enormous funds for Jammu and Kashmir, but a high percentage of these funds went into the consolidation of military power at the lines of control.

The mid-1960s also saw the emergence of the armed militants of the Jammu and Kashmir National Liberation Front, and the beginnings of skirmishes between such groups and security forces, which continued into the next decade. Even when, or perhaps particularly when, Sheikh Abdullah and Prime Minister Indira Gandhi signed an accord in 1974 that was widely considered to represent an understanding that no plebiscite would ever be called for and that Jammu and Kashmir was to be considered a constituent state in the Indian Union, these armed militants began to capture the imagination of Kashmiris and to represent an unlikely force for change. Another turning point came in the rigged elections of 1987, when candidates of the Muslim United Front, who spoke in the name of freedom and Islam, were arrested or sidelined in order to let a National Conference-Congress alliance come to power. Several of these candidates, now convinced that Indian democracy did not extend to Kashmiris, left to join armed militant groups operating out of Pakistan. Not long after, violent attacks and bombings became a regular feature in Kashmir. Pakistani support for militant camps in Azad Kashmir meant that larger groups of young Kashmiris (from both sides of the border) as well as veterans of the anti-Soviet war in Afghanistan could swell the ranks of anti-India militants. If the idea of Kashmiris armed and willing enough to take on far superior military forces came as an unwelcome surprise for Indians and for the Indian political establishment, the popular support the militants enjoyed, so many years after the accession of the state in 1947, was quite stunning. Few Indians or mainstream politicians had paid attention to the uneasy history of the accession as well as the continuing history of undemocratic functioning in the state. Not surprisingly, there was little by way of imaginative political or administrative response to these new circumstances. The government machinery simply fought back: from 1990 onward, the Indian army and paramilitary forces clamped down, and, squeezed between the militants and the military, Kashmiri lives descended into the misery and brutality I have already described.

In this section I have called attention to three elements that structure the Kashmir problem: the history of Kashmiri Muslim alienation from a de facto Hindu state, the long tentacles of the Partition of India, whose malignant grasp allows for no conception of political collectivity not defined by the fortified borders of India and Pakistan, and the gross and widespread violations of human rights that have defined Kashmiri lives for two decades now. It has been clear for some years now that armed insurgency will not lead to any resolution of the Kashmir conflict (estimates suggest that no more than a few hundred militants are still active). However, even as the militancy has been contained, the anger and disaffection of Kashmiris is far from dissipated. Even with an elected state government in place, massive strikes and protests recur across Kashmir, and local resistance is often orchestrated by stone-throwing young men (Bukhari 2010; Kak 2011).

For many military and civil administrators, political resistance is now simply a problem of law and order, to be sorted out through displays of force. However, the continuing intensity of the protests—even when they are sporadic—and indeed of the state response, is such that many Indian civil society groups, journalists, and important politicians have focused their attention on the ongoing conflict in Kashmir. Even centrist intellectuals have called for the repeal of the Armed Forces Special Powers Act (AFSPA), which allows virtual impunity to officers and soldiers, and the Public Safety Act (PSA), which allows police to detain individuals up to two years without charge or trial. No progress along these lines has been made; senior army officers made statements insisting they could not function without the legal cover provided by the AFSPA, and the PSA continues to be routinely used to imprison people.[5] There is much evidence now that various organs of the Indian state function at odds with each other vis-à-vis Kashmir—elected officials are distrusted by their military and police counterparts, the central paramilitaries are often at odds with the state police, and even the central Home and Defence Ministries do not agree about weighty matters like troop deployment in civilian areas. The situation remains as polarized as ever.

The future—certainly the possibility of a political resolution of the problem of Kashmir—looks bleak. India grows increasingly powerful economically and militarily, and its aspirations toward regional superpower status means that its strategic planners will deny any possibility of self-determination for Kashmiris. Pakistan, bloodied internally by militants and religious insurgents, needs more than ever to demonstrate its commitment to a muscular nationalism the equal of India's, and will continue to treat Azad Kashmir as a captive launching pad for actions against Indian Kashmir. Kashmiris themselves are a deeply divided people, and not just because most Kashmiri Hindus no longer live among their Muslim neighbors in the valley. Kashmiri Muslims too are divided by denominational differences and political loyalties. In any case the idea of Kashmir, even for proponents of self-determination today, is often ill-defined, for it is based on a demand for the independence of an erstwhile territorial entity artificially crafted to suit the interests of the British Empire. Ironically, the insistence on an independent Jammu and Kashmir is based on a refusal to acknowledge that large populations in Jammu and Ladakh had made clear that they wish to remain Indians. For them, the Kashmiri demand for independence amounts to an invitation to a reiterated partition that will, at worst, reiterate the bloodshed and population movements of 1947.

Today, few Kashmiris trust governmental or civil society organizations (even as many are employed by them), for so many of them have turned out to be tainted, to be vehicles for the extension of state surveillance or patronage. As I mentioned earlier, government agencies also created or exploited schisms between militant groups, and they were particularly successful at turning captured militants against their own, till the *ikhwanis* (which is what renegade militants were called locally) became a byword for cruelty against their own people. Some argue that the state's sponsorship of the ikhwanis did more to tear apart Kashmiri society than even the direct actions of soldiers. Their local knowledge was such that their ruthless actions were particularly intimate betrayals of their communities. They destroyed long-shared ties, and the legacy of their brutality still separates people. And of course no Kashmiri escaped the enhanced surveillance, the random searches, the checkpoints, and bunkers that defined everyday life.

CREATIVITY AND POLITICAL LIFE

Life in Kashmir continues to be burdened in ways that few outsiders can imagine. For the last twenty-five years Kashmiris have been on a wild and dangerous roller-coaster ride, high hopes giving way to depths of despair. Mourning and anger go hand in hand now, each fueling political rage against their treatment by India. Two decades of trauma and loss have caused many to question how long they can afford to resist state power, but equally, this period has seen the coming into adulthood of a generation of young people who have known no other lives, and are thereby confirmed in their political opposition. They take to the streets on occasion, but they have also found other powerful ways of expressing their discontent and their hopes. In novels, in poetry, in films, and in documentary prose, they perform the psychic as well as the urgent political and cultural dislocations they have experienced. Their creativity insists upon the importance of everyday experience in any analyses of history and politics; thinking with and through these texts becomes one way to refuse to depopulate historical explanation or to analyze politics and national security as if people do not matter.

In this volume I have collected poems that do such work, but poetry is of course far from the only medium that articulates social suffering, and recent memoirs, novels, and plays make available the realities of Kashmiri lives under occupation, till today no one can claim that they are unaware of all that is happening in Kashmir. Equally, the complexities of affiliation and belonging, of resistance and survival, mapped in such writing are a challenge to doctrinaire definitions of freedom articulated by leaders of the Kashmiri tehreek. Further, civil society groups and academics have been producing evidence of the effects of long-term violence in Kashmir, ranging from lists of the disappeared and of the large number of unmarked mass graves to reports on the high incidence of mental illness and drug addiction. Journalists and documentary filmmakers have in turn recorded testimonials of torture at the hands of security forces, and feature films on similar themes have recently been completed. Similarly, there are novels, short stories, and documentary films that explore the predicament of Kashmiri Hindus in exile for two and a half decades now, and their deep ambivalence about, and fear of, returning home.[6]

For young Kashmiris, such critical and cultural work has in fact become a crucial form of activism, particularly in a period when it is increasingly clear that India's growing economic and military power and its capacity to silence whatever meager international attention is paid to Kashmir seem to close off all paths to political self-determination. Whatever "progress" is made on Kashmir now takes the form of governmental commissions and committees that produce reports on how to effect tepid administrative reforms. At their most radical, these reports remind the central government that, post the signing of the Instrument of Accession in 1947, a crucial amendment to the Indian constitution guaranteed certain functional autonomies to the state of Jammu and Kashmir. Thus, the only viable "solutions" at this point seem to be those contained within the constitutional provisions, and the highly policed territorial boundaries, of India.

In this political impasse, there exists an acute need to record events, to commemorate losses and occasional victories, to revise received historical narratives, and also to explore possibilities ahead. And all of this creativity takes place in a context where there is no escaping the fact that no one who writes on Kashmir can do so without her own identity being invoked to celebrate or denounce the ideas they explore. In a situation where your name makes clear your religious affiliation, no byline is exempt from such scrutiny. Further, the experiences of the last two decades have so defined political positions in and about Kashmir that most local analysts—Hindus and Muslims—begin by calling attention to all that they have seen and known, and then go on to detail how these experiences shape their political and historical understanding. They do not only report trauma, of course; many write of acts of great kindness and love across supposedly impassable divides, and a great many Muslims and Hindus mourn the loss of shared lives, and insist on the primary challenge of restoring almost disappeared ties between communities.

Such writing often invokes multiple temporalities—a comparatively benign, sometimes romanticized past, the difficult present, an imagined better future—which means that its range effectively constitutes a history of the land and its peoples. These records of the experiences, frustrations, and aspirations of people are in fact the archives that should shape our historiographical concerns, and cause us to re-examine our analytic fixation with state policies and institutions, national interests, and international relations. Of course, any serious writing on a situation like Kashmir cannot dispense with the latter, but equally, it should be impossible for any commentator to side-step the politically formative power of everyday experience and indeed of the powerful memories they generate. In many ways then, this new corpus of creativity and discussion is a more promising archive for any study of Kashmiri consciousness (political and otherwise) in the present moment than exclusively state-centric conversations about security, governance, or even development.[7]

....

In the next chapter, I discuss the need for us to attend to such creativity at much greater length, but here I want to close with a song that became an anthem of resistance and mourning in 2010. This is the Srinagar-based rapper MC Kash's "I Protest (Remembrance)."[8] This rap too invokes a longer history of crisis: the unfulfilled promise of a plebiscite and the ongoing public skepticism about the fairness of "democratically held elections." Most pressingly however, he repeatedly calls attention to atrocities and repression, but also, tellingly, to the national media that Kashmiris so mistrust, the "Sponsored Media Who Hide This Homicide." The last sequence of the song has the rapper intoning the names of those who were shot by the time he wrote it, and this (incomplete) list is chilling, a memorial to the young mowed down by police actions. MC Kash's combination of protest and remembrance, indictment and memorialization, anger and sorrow, is powerful testimonial to the Kashmiri suffering that shapes its politics today, as is the pledge with which he closes: "An' You Will Fight, Till The Death Of It. . . ."

They Say When You Run From Darkness All You Seek Is Light.
But When The Blood Spills Over You'll Stand And Fight!!
Threads Of Deceit Woven Around A Word Of Plebiscite, By
Treacherous Puppet Politicians Who Have No Soul Inside.
My Paradise Is Burnin' With Troops Left Loose With Ammo,
Who Murder And Rape Then Hide Behind A Political Shadow.
Like A Casino Human Life Is Thrown Like A Dice, I'll Summarize
Atrocities Till The Resurrection Of Christ!!!
Can You Hear The Screams Now See The Revolution!! Their
Bullets Our Stones, Don't Talk Restitution.
'Cause The Only Solution Is The Resolution Of Freedom, Even
Khusrow Will Go Back An' Doubt his Untimely Wisdom!!
These Killings Ain't Random Its An Organized Genocide. Sponsored
Media Who Hide This Homicide.
No More Injustice We Wont Go Down When We Bleed, Alive In
The Struggle Even The Graves Will Speak!

Chorus: I Protest, Against The Things You Done! I Protest, For A
Mother Who Lost Her Son!
I Protest, I'll Throw Stones And Neva Run! I Protest, Until My
Freedom Has Come!
I Protest, For My Brother Who's Dead! I Protest, Against The
Bullet In his Head!
I Protest, I'll Throw Stones And Neva Run! I Protest, Until My
Freedom Has Come!

Democratically Held Elections Now That's Completely Absurd,
I'll Tell You Some Stuff That You Obviously Neva Heard!!
A Ten Year Old Kid Voted With All his Fingers. A Whole Village
Gang Raped, A Cry Still Lingers. . . .
These Are The Tales From The Dark Side Of A Murderous Regime,
An Endless Occupation Of Our Land An' Our Dreams.
Democratic Politics Will Cut Our Throats Before We Speak, How
They Talk About Peace When There's Blood In Our Streets?
(huh?)
When Freedom Of Speech Is Subjected To Strangulation!!
Flames Of Revolution Engulfs The Population.
They Rise Through Suppression And March To Be Free, Face

Covered in A Rag Labeled A Revolutionary.
Through This Fight For Survival I Want The World To See, A
Murderous Oppression Written Down In Police Brutality.
Stones In My Hand It's Time You Pay The Price, For Plunderin'
An' Rapin' A Beautiful Paradise!!

Chorus: I Protest, Against The Things You Done! I Protest, For A
Mother Who Lost Her Son!
I Protest, I'll Throw Stones And Neva Run! I Protest, Until My
Freedom Has Come!
I Protest, For My Brother Who's Dead! I Protest, Against The
Bullet In his Head!
I Protest, I'll Throw Stones And Neva Run! I Protest, Until My
Freedom Has Come!

Lets Remember All Those Who Were Martyred This Year.
Inayat Khan, Wamiq Farooq, Zahid Farooq, Zubair Ahmed Bhat,
Tufail Ahmed Matoo, Rafiq Ahmed Bangroo, Javaid Ahmed Malla,
Shakeel Ganai, Firdous Khan, Bilal Ahmed Wani, Tajamul Bashir,
Tauqeer Rather, Ishtiyaq Ahmed, Imtiyaz Ahmed Itoo, Shujaat-ul-
Islaam, Muzaffar Ahmed, Fayaz Ahmed Wani, Yasmeen Jan, Abrar
Ahmed Khan, Faizan Rafeeq, Fayaz Ahmed Khanday, Farooq
Ahmed, Tariq Ahmed Dar, Mohammed Ahsan, Showkat Ahmed,
Mohammed Rafiq, Nazir Ahmed, Javed Ahmed Teli, Mudassir
Lone, Nayeem Shah, Rayees Wani, Afrooza Teli, Basharat Reshi,
Irshad Bhat, Ashiq Hussain, Rameez Ahmed, Hafiz Yaqoob, Tariq
Dar, Khursheed Ahmed, Bashir Ahmed Reshi, Arshid Ahmad,
Sameer Rah, Mehraj ud din Lone, Anis Ganai, Suhail Ahmed Dar,
Jehangir Baht, Riyaz Ahmed, Mohammad Yaqoob Bhat, Iqbal
Khan, Shabir Malik, Ghulam Nabi Badyari, Rameez Reshi, Fida
Nabi Lone, Farrukh Bukhari, Mudassir Zargar, Ali Mohammad
Khanday, Asif Mir, Sameer Lone, Umar Ahmed Dar, Irshad Ahmed,
Mohammad Abbas, Milad Ahmed Dar, Nazir Wani, Mudasir Nazir,
Bilal Ahmed Sheikh, Umar Qayoom, Irshad Ahmad.

An' You Will Fight, Till The Death Of It. . . .

1. The term *intifada* is one that the Kashmiri *sangbaaz* (stone pelters) have made their own. The problem of Kashmir does not map exactly on to the Israeli occupation of Palestine, but young Kashmiris see the style of revolt—young men with stones, often masked in *keffiyehs*, facing up to soldiers with arms—as inspirational. This is not only an issue of style, of course, but also of parallel historical genealogies, since both the Israel-Palestine conflict and the India-Kashmir-Pakistan imbroglio were the direct result of British colonial officers partitioning territories without any understanding of or concern for local populations (Cleary 2002).

2. Junagarh and Hyderabad, two Princely States with Muslim rulers and a majority Hindu population, provide a counterpoint to Kashmir (both these states were territorially contained within India; only Kashmir shared borders with both India and Pakistan). The ruler of Junagarh sought to accede to Pakistan; an Indian blockade caused him to flee, and the state's amalgamation with India was ratified in a plebiscite conducted in February 1948. The nizam of Hyderabad wavered between independence and accession to Pakistan, but was removed from power by the Indian Army in a "police action" in September 1948.

3. These numbers, as is the case with all those connected with Partition deaths and dislocations, are impressionistic. For a careful examination (and estimation) of this problem of numbers, see Corruccini and Kaul. In their analysis of Punjab, they write:

> Several methods of estimating total Partition mortality (both in present-day Pakistan and India) point to a *maximum* of perhaps about 400,000 ± 100,000 deaths. Of these about a third were violent deaths in the first days of attacks, and most of the remainder were cholera along the migration track or various illnesses of poor public sanitation in the early camps. (1990: 37)

4. Cabeiri Robinson's *Body of Victim, Body of Warrior: Refugee Families and the Making of Kashmiri Jihadists* is a consequential study of the participation of ex-citizens of the princely state of Jammu and Kashmir, now "refugees" in Pakistan-administered areas, in the politics of these disputed regions as well as in armed actions against the Indian state both before and after 1989.

5. Margaret Sekaggya, the United Nations Special Rapporteur on the Situation of Human Rights Defenders, has, after a recent visit to Kashmir, demanded the repeal of these laws (see "Begin Healing Process" 2011).

6. Some instances of such creativity are Siddhartha Gigoo and Varad Sharma, eds. *A Long Dream of Home: The Persecution, Exodus and Exile of Kashmiri Pandits*, Rahul Pandita's memoir *Our Moon has Blood Clots*, Mirza Waheed's novels, *The Book of Gold Leaves* and, *The Collaborator*, Siddhartha Gigoo's novel, *The Garden of Solitude*, Basharat Peer's memoir, *Curfewed Night*, and the essays collected in Fahad Shah, ed. *Of Occupation and Resistance* and Sanjay Kak, ed. *Until My Freedom Has Come*. Ira Pande, ed. *A Tangled Web: Jammu & Kashmir* contains articles that offer stark examples of the contrast between the vocabulary of Indian policymakers and that of Kashmiris who have suffered the violence of the state. Sanjay Kak's 2008 documentary, *Jashn-e-Azadi: How We*

Celebrate Freedom, was the first to explore the militarization of daily life in Kashmir. Ajay Raina's *Apour ti Yapour* (2011) and *Paradise on a River of Hell* (2002) directed by Abir Bazaz and Meenu Gaur, explore similar themes. A few filmmakers have also produced feature-length movies: Musa Sayeed, *Valley of Saints* (2012); Aamir Bashir, *Harud* (2010); and Tariq Tapa, *Zero Bridge* (2008). Also worth listening to is Roushan Illahi, who raps in English as MC Kash: http://www.mckashofficial.com (accessed on January 13, 2014). An important volume of poetry in English to have emerged from this conflict is Agha Shahid Ali's *The Country without a Post Office*.

7. One example of the analysis of public events and performances that demand a voice in Kashmiri politics is to be found in Deepti Misri's account of the demonstrations staged in parks by the Association of Parents of Disappeared Persons (APDP), as well as her analysis of activist art in Srinagar. See her chapter, "'This Is Not a Performance!' Public Mourning and Visual Spectacle in Kashmir," in *Beyond Partition: Gender, Violence, and Representation in Postcolonial India*, 133–60.

8. The full force of this rap becomes clear when it is heard (http://www.mckashofficial .com/the-vault). The song, overlaid with images from the summer's protests, is also available on YouTube: http://www.youtube.com/watch?v=DFDrRaLcUvQ).

Moti Lal "Saqi"

Savāl

Hu ti akh ādam
Tsi ti akh ādam
Ba̱ ti akh ādam

Kani mā kānh phoṭ nabu' mā kānh voth
Talpatālu' ti kānh mā hẙor khot
Sā̱rī mẙśimiri māji zāy
Teli asi bẙn kus dūrẙr tshẙn kus
Tali sa̱ tseth dith sā̱rī sūciv
Mẙ che zan sōcas phạṭmu'ts lāy

Pōś rangarang bāghas yāvun
Makhma̱li nīli voẕu'li so̱nhạri
Os nu' gulālas kā̱nsi ti dāghan

Gō nu' go̱lābas bram kho̱śbōyuk
Kor nā anār ẙv śarmandu' jāfar
Brēḍi zānh thẙok ni zi sārẙn ziuṭh chus
Āyi ya̱mbu'rzal lōnci lamẙs kus
Masvali ḍar chu nu' kunizani paknas
Kongpōśan zānh ka̱r nu' mo̱lu'j kath
Lājvarsi duśman chuni sōsan
Thanival āyi ti tsạj potkho̱rī
Kōtā miūṭh yihund tsho̱ṭ dunyā
So̱khu' samsār tu' chu nu' nẙāy

Tīr khẙolā khot dorān bālas
Nāba̱di kā̱tẙah kātsir kū'ti
Kā̱tẙah ciṭu' krehniārchu kūtẙn
Nayi nayi phērān tshālu' divān
Yikvaṭu' sā̱rī vū'nd dini nērān
Yikvaṭu' sā̱rī kāsān trēś

Moti Lal "Saqi"

Question

He too is a man
You too are a man
I too am a man

No one sprung up from rock, no one dropped from the sky
No one climbed up from the underworld either
All are as clay, are born to mothers
Then who amongst us is separate, who torn apart by distance
Let's then think consciously all of us—
I seem to have burst the kernels of my thought

Flowers many-colored, the garden bloomed
Velvet, blue, red, golden
No one needed to slit the poppy

The rose did not become arrogant about its perfume
The pomegranate did not shame the marigold
The pussy willow did not boast though it blossomed first
The narcissus comes, who will drag it down
The iris has no fear of walking alone
The saffron flower never spoke its value
The violet knows no enemy in the lily
The shy thaniwal grew, back-tracked, and eased away
How sweet their little world
Peaceful world,[1] there is no quarrel

Flocks of sheep run up the hillside
Crystal-colored how many, how many cream
How many white, blackish how many
Wandering in valleys, bounding about

Rōm karān chunu' aḍu'khẙv tūsis
Kātsur cīrinu' krihnis hoṭ
Hāris nābaḍi chunu' khrẙku'nāvān

Talsā pritshtav panu'nis pānas
Asi insānan kav bad rāy?

All together they go out to graze
All together they slake their thirst
No harm comes to the underfed ram
The creamy one will not squeeze the black's neck
The crystal does not frighten the mottled one

Then just ask a question of yourselves
Why do we humans have bad thoughts?

....

Published in *Sheeraza* (Kashmiri) 29:4 (1994), 92.

Moti Lal "Saqi" (1936–1999) was born in Mahanoor Chadoora, Budgam. He matriculated
from the Government School Chraar and later completed a BA degree. He wrote poetry
and plays, collected folklore, and translated both literary criticism and philosophy, for
which he won awards from the State Cultural Academy as well as the Padma Shri (1989).

NOTE

1. The poet uses "duniya" in one line and "samsara" in the other to show that words
derived from Arabic and words derived from Sanskrit coexist as synonyms in Kashmiri.

Mohiuddin "Massarat"

Ghazal

Khūn chu prēṛān athan mỷ kiā
Han han chu dazān badan mỷ kiā

Lot lot chu pakān vāti yi kot
Siriyi chu lōsān vatan mỷ kiā

Kami kor van sậ kanḍỷn pēvand
Chinu' zi phọlān caman mỷ kiā

Vuṭh chi pheśān khayāl matiō
Oś chu vasān palan mỷ kiā

Vạdi vạdi ậnu' chu vuchān
Vyup chu khasān ậchan mỷ kiā

Chi banān panu'ni vọpar gāhē
Māz chu vọthān naman mỷ kiā

Che zabān kalān vach chu khamān
Chu mā'ni ḍalān kathan mỷ kiā

Ādam chu marān kiā chu sarān
Massarat chu gindān ghaman mỷ kiā

Mohiuddin "Massarat"

Ghazal

Blood drips from hands, what's to me?
Bit by bit the body burns, what's to me?

Slowly, slowly it walks, where might it reach?
The sun is meandering lost on paths, what's to me?

Who, tell me, made grafts of these thorns?
So the gardens do not flower, what's to me?

Lips quiver to speak thoughts, *matyov*
Tears flow from boulders, what's to me?

The mirror weeps and weeps and watches![1]
The eyes are flooding, what's to me?

Our own become strangers sometime
Flesh is pulling off nails, what's to me?[2]

The tongue stutters, the chest heaves
The meanings of words shift, what's to me?

Adam is dying, what does he observe?[3]
Massarat[4] plays with sorrows, what's to me?

· · · · · · · · · · · · · · · ·

Published in *Sheeraza* (Kashmiri) 38:3–5 (2006), 198.

Mohiuddin "Massarat" was born in 1945 in Fateh Kadal, Srinagar. He was schooled locally in Bab Demb, worked in the Public Works Department and retired as a senior clerk. He writes poetry and presents his work on Radio Kashmir and on television, as well as in programs sponsored by the Cultural Academy.

1. The syntax of the original line can also suggest a person weeping and watching (himself) in the mirror. This line thus links the "tears" of inanimate objects like boulders or mirrors to human eyes that flood with tears.

2. In Kashmiri, *nam te maaz* (nails and flesh) is an idiomatic phrase used to suggest closeness—between brother and sister, for instance, or the closest of friends. Here, following upon the previous line, "Our own become strangers," the literalization of this metaphor (flesh pulled off nails) suggests torture, which brutalizes not only the individual body but also tears apart the family and the community.

3. *Adam* here is mankind; his dying the death of all.

4. *Massarat*, the poet's *takhallus* (pen name), means happiness.

Policemen throw stones at demonstrators during a protest in Maisuma | Srinagar,
June 2009

Mir Ghulam Nabi "Shaheen"

Tsu' āēkh?

Tsu' āēkh pān pāṛāvith amā poz
Dilak hāvas mẙ vuphārāvith amā poz
Lachan āyakh tsu' dafnāvith amā poz
Patō tshẙph dith tsajikh trāvith amā poz

Mẙ mandinyn śām gō bāras sapun poḥ
Tsu' chakh mārān ghāran sū'thi az tshoḥ

Mẙ zōnum cāni yinu' mẙ dāg tsalnam
Gāmit vūjāru'h sāṛī bāg pholnam
Yiyam śāyad mẙ fursath dād balnam
Mẙ cāvan ābi kōsar 'ātu'r malnam

Vomēzan manz kaṛān chus rāth ty doḥ
Tsu' chakh mārān ghāran sū'thi az tshoḥ

Kamō diut khūn kam gay khānu' vujār
Kamō vali vali kafan ōs gyundmut zār
Kaman vathi mu'ti bicāṛẙn talpadẙn pār
Tihu'nz kunu' chā kathā vuchtav sā akhbār

Kamō sanglāt tsaṭimu'ti prātmu'ti koḥ
Tsu' chakh mārān ghāran sū'th az tshoḥ

Qasam chum cāni 'zmatu'kuy vanday rath
Vanu'n cham mokhtasar pāṭhẙn mẙ akh kath
Kun naẕrah karukh sārinī bu' hẙth
Che pinhā tath andar bas cāni qodrath

Tsu' chakh zālān tomul zālun tse chuy toḥ
Tsu' chakh mārān ghāran sū'thi az tshoḥ

Mir Ghulam Nabi "Shaheen"

You Came?

You came all dressed up, true enough
My heart's desire you excited, true enough
You came after burying thousands, true enough
Then, surreptitiously, you ran away from me, true enough

My days turned to evening, summer turned winter
You are off gallivanting with strangers today

I had thought that your coming will remove my hurt
All my ruined gardens will blossom
Perhaps I will find some rest, my pains will heal
I will be offered the waters of Kausar,[1] perfumes applied

In hopes I pass my night and day
You are off gallivanting with strangers today

All who gave blood, which homes were ruined
All who, wrapped in shrouds, played with risk
All who, poor ones, have lost the skin of their soles
Is there talk of them anywhere, take a look at the newspapers

All who cut through rocks, dug through mountains
You are off gallivanting with strangers today

I swear by your grandeur, I pledge you my blood
I wish to speak, in brief, a word
Look as one upon everyone, including me
Concealed in just that is your grace.

You are burning rice, you should be burning chaff
You are off gallivanting with strangers today

Published in *Sheeraza* (Kashmiri) 27:5 (1993), 107–08.

Mir Ghulam Nabi "Shaheen" was born in Sanoor Kali Pora, Beerwah in 1942. He took his MA in Kashmiri and history from Kashmir University and worked in the state Education Department. He writes on Kashmiri history and culture, and is the founder of a cultural forum, Bazm-e-Adab, Batapora. He recently published *Hub-e-Hazoor* (a collection of *Na'ats*).

NOTE

1. It is said that those who are admitted to *Jannat* (Paradise) will drink the water of the cistern of Kausar.

During curfew, a child peers through a window in his home | Srinagar, March 2009

Jawahir Lal "Saroor"

Ghazal

Krẙkh vạts lāru'c dār hiotun nār khabardār
Kathi kathi gọbiōmut bār zan talvār khabardār

Partsẙni gạtshit az pōśi nūlan rạv chapan jāi
Chī pośi tharẙn pẙṭh basān ṣạhmār khabardār

Ratu' dạvi nālas voni cha lẙkhit mẙạn gudran kath
Kani kani mẙ pānay pān kor sangsār khabardār

Mạhlam pacav kor nu' asar dag cha hurạnī
Ang ang chu tshaṭān nār khabardār khabardār

Dẙvānkhānan manz chi karān rātu'mọghal rāj
Prẙth kōci gạlis pẙṭh lẙkhit iśtẙār khabardār

Āmun chu āmut rāyi nīras Vẙth cha phēśān vuṭh
Vāvas chu tavay az badal anhār khabardār

Jawahir Lal "Saroor"

Ghazal

Cries arose everywhere, fire raged, be warned
So much is heavier, like a sword, be warned

Torn and alone, the orioles have lost their shelter
On boughs of flowers are living great serpents, be warned

On my bloodstained collar still is written the story of my tragedy
With stones upon stones I have battered myself, be warned

Soothing dressings have had no effect, the pain increases
Limb upon limb winnows flames, be warned, be warned

In drawing rooms the night-owls rule
At every lane end is posted a notice, be warned

Smells of burning come from the meadows, the Vyeth's lips are parched
That's why the wind has a different face today, be warned.

....

Published in *Sheeraza* (Kashmiri), 31:4 (1997), 127.

Jawahir Lal "Saroor" was born in 1939 in Mahanoor Chadora. He studied at the Shopian
High School, did a Basic Education Course in 1957, completed a B.Ed. and later an MA
in Kashmiri. He taught in government schools and retired in 1989. He has published
several books, and his writing has been translated into many languages.

Pyare "Hatash"

Ghazal

Nazar nazar vuhān seki śāṭh
Taraf taraf zuvān seki śāṭh

Qatu'l, ghāratgōrī yi kiā sapun
Adu'l insāf ḍuvān seki śāṭh

Yi kus mūd tay hu kas mōrukh
Tsavapāri kafan suvān seki śāṭh

Mandōrẙn quluf vạhi baskīn nābōd
Kus kạmis sạti tsuvān seki śāṭh

Chu basti sūr pholmut vuch Hatāś
Datur purnẙn ruvān seki śāṭh

Pyare "Hatash"

Ghazal

Gaze upon gaze scorches desert sands
In every direction are born desert sands

Murder, plunder, what's this that has been gifted
Law and justice are swept away—desert sands

Who is it that died, who is it that was killed
Everywhere shrouds are stitched—desert sands

Mansions locked, alas the inhabitants are nowhere
Who fights with whom—desert sands

Hamlets bloom into ash, look, *Hatash*
Datura[1] is sown in plots, desert sands

....

Published in *Sheeraza* (Kashmiri) 31:6 (1997), 65.

Pyare Lal Handoo, who took the pen name "Hatash," was born in 1948 in Anantnag. He has MA degrees in Urdu and Hindi and was in government service until he retired. Of his many publications, *Karb-e-Wajood, Lamhaat-i-Gumshudah, Gardish-i-Ayaam* and *Yaad-e-Zaafran* are well known.

NOTE

1. *Datura* is a genus of poisonous and hallucinogenic flowering plants.

Ghulam Nabi "Khayal"

Fariyād

Yus kadam sẙzruk tujōv tạthi gov hajar yā Mustafā[S.A.W.]
Kặśris qōmas karakh nā akh naẓar yā Mustafā[S.A.W.]

Zāl bọnu' vạhrukh tanābav sū'ti cōrukh āsmān
Vuḍvu'nẙn jānāvaran phuṭimiti chi par yā Mustafā[S.A.W.]

Yanu' yiman sānẙn baran śạstu'r ṣadā gạy tang phuṭikh
Vọni khọtẙn manz tsūri chuy sōruy śahar yā Mustafā[S.A.W.]

Sūri gov pōnpur śama vẙgliōv tu' du'hi tshẙtu'rāt gạy
Gāś tshiōv gạṭi gēru' kor phọli kar saḥar yā Mustafā[S.A.W.]

Tsặngi tshẙtu' gạy rang chatiāy kath pōśi bani suru' ḍēr gov
Mulki Kaśmīras yi lạji kạmisu'nz naẓar yā Mustafā[S.A.W.]

Śọngnu' bronh yeli rāth khāki pā tuhund caśman mothum
Sāsu' bạdi tārakh vuchim khābas andar yā Mustafā[S.A.W.]

Ghulam Nabi "Khayal"

Appeal

Those righteous steps we took, those went astray, Ya Mustafa[S.A.W.]
Will you not cast a glance at the Kashmiri people, Ya Mustafa[S.A.W.]

They spread webs below, with ropes they tightened the sky
The wings of flying birds have broken, Ya Mustafa[S.A.W.]

Since iron-sounds were heard on our doors, hinges are broken
Now the entire city is concealed in hideaways, Ya Mustafa[S.A.W.]

The moth became cinders, the candle melted, and the night turned
                                                    smoky-close
Light dimmed, the dark fell around, when will the dawn bloom,
                                            Ya Mustafa[S.A.W.]

Oil-lamps were snuffed, colours paled, piles of flowers turned heaps of ash
Whose evil eye has blighted the nation of Kashmir, Ya Mustafa[S.A.W.]

Last night, before I slept, when I rubbed the dust of your feet on my eyes
I saw thousands of stars in my dream, Ya Mustafa[S.A.W.]

....

Published in *Sheeraza* (Kashmiri) 40:1–3 (2007), 121.

Meer Ghulam Nabi "Khayal" was born in 1939. He has published twenty-eight books in Kashmiri, Urdu, and English and has edited weeklies in each of these languages. He has been awarded the Sahitya Akademi award (1975) and the Jammu and Kashmir Cultural Academy award for writing in both Kashmiri (1974) and English (2010).

NOTE

This poem is formally a *Na'at*, a praise-song addressed to the Prophet, which contains an appeal for his intervention.

"Shahzada" Rafiq

Ghazal

Mẙāni śahruk nafar nafar khāmōś
Siryi śāphal nazar nazar khāmōś

Rãts caśman kazul vudạsī hund
Dọh chu phẙśal qahar qahar khāmōś

Zūni zūtan vaṭu'si tu' siriyas tām
Dāghu' niōmut jigar jigar khāmōś

Gām gãyil ạchav vuchān karbal
Mẙōn āngun tu' dāri bar khāmōś

Rōṭu' gãmu'ts vunal vaṭu'si vatu' gath
Vāv vẙvrān zahar zahar khāmōś

Thām gãmu't vurēbu' samyiki kuli
Sīnu' prãṭith qabar qabar khāmōś

Yath makānas andar apuz vẙvhār
Bōḍ lẙkhit pazar pazar khāmōś

"Shahzada" Rafiq

Ghazal

In my city person after person is silent
The cursed sun—sight upon sight is silent

The eyes of night wear the kohl of sadness
The day ominous, wrecked—even wrecks are silent

The moon's light is petrified, the sun blighted
Beaten down the heart—even hearts[1] are silent

Wounded villages, eyes seeing Karbala
My yard and windows and doors are silent

The fog immobilized, trails in alleyways
The wind sows poison—even poison is silent

Stunted, upside-down are the trees of time
Ripped-open graves—even graves are silent

Inside this house, lying is the norm
Writ large the truth—but truth is silent.

....

Published in *Sheeraza* (Kashmiri), 27:2 (1993), 84.

NOTE

1. The Kashmiri phrase is *jigar jigar*, which literally means "liver, liver." This idiomatic phrase does not translate exactly into English, and the closest equivalent is "heart."

A protester throws stones at paramilitary soldiers and police | Srinagar,
January 2009

Essay 3

The Witness of Poetry

Political Feeling in Kashmiri Poems

Concertina wire is the most widespread form of vegetation in Kashmir today. It grows everywhere, including in the mind.

—RANJIT HOSKOTE 2011: lxxiii.

Kashmir has seen extraordinary violence over the last two decades, and much of it has been documented by Kashmiri and international human rights groups, civil society activists, and journalists. However the effect such long-term violence has had in the forging of political subjectivities has not become central to scholarship on contemporary Kashmir. That Kashmir has become a conflict zone, with periods of intense violence followed by months of relative calm, is acknowledged by all, but commentators rarely factor in the effects of such prolonged instability and suffering on the political and social attitudes of Kashmiris today. Analysts tend to focus on political developments and incidents of violence in the moment, and even those who recognize that there is an entire generation and more whose only sense of "normality" is of a conflict-ridden Kashmir, make this observation only to set it aside. Noticeably absent from such analyses is a sense of traumatized lives under siege, or of the way in which the pressure of events transforms subjectivities and repurposes political priorities over time.[1]

But loss and traumatic experiences are now woven into the fabric of Kashmiri lives: everyone has first-hand accounts of violence to offer, and people often call attention to their experiences as they explain their political positions. In earlier chapters, I have suggested that creative texts produced in times of conflict offer a way of addressing crucial lacunae in our understanding of Kashmir and Kashmiris, for they illuminate not only the political and ideological issues at stake, but also states of being precipitated by violence, loss, and resistance. For instance, poems from conflict zones are sure guides to the intensity of feelings that result from prolonged conflicts, and which, over time, play a significant role in the perpetuation of the conflict. This can be a matter of idiom and tone, for the performative elements of a poem emphasize emotional and psychological intensities sidelined in the affectively neutral tones of news reportage, policy documents, or standard historiography. As Muzamil Jaleel noted early in the period of conflict, Kashmiri poetry had become a crucial medium for the articulation of trauma and of protest in a time when censorship and fear made writing in prose dangerous (2002).

In recent years I have been working with a Srinagar-based scholar to collect and translate contemporary poetry in Kashmiri into English. Our project is particular: we ask how poets have responded to the bloody disruption of civic and political order in Kashmir in the last two decades. As we know, poets are artisans who are bound by past practices (formal and generic conventions, arresting images or turns of phrase, powerful insights into existential or historical conditions) even as they generate innovations in theme and language that allow them to engage with the present in order to imagine different futures. Poems, that is, can be read as bearing witness to, or more precisely, *performing*, the fracturing or forging of cultural assumptions. In Kashmir, poems have provided a remarkable number of everyday colloquialisms and aphorisms, and have thus long played an important role in the historical formation of *Kashmiriyat*, the idea of a collectivity different from others outside the language community. For instance, phrases and lines from the poems of the fourteenth-century mystics Lal Dĕd and Sheikh Noor-ud-din Wali (Nund Rishi) are treated as maxims, and spoken often enough to constitute the commonsense of the land.[2]

While *Kashmiriyat* as idea and as description of shared lives and cultural assumptions across religious communities has been belittled as a utopian, retrospective backformation that attempts to paper over age-old sectarian and social divides, there is no question that the melding of Buddhist, Hindu, and Muslim ideals provided Kashmiris with a vast reservoir of spiritual ideas at odds with more doctrinaire and prescriptive forms of religious belief. Many of these ideas are central to the Sufi tradition, with its concomitant devotion to local shrines, that differentiates both Muslim and Hindu forms of worship in Kashmir from practices elsewhere (not seamlessly or without contestation, of course, but certainly definitively). Thus, the disappearance of crucial elements of this way of life—the loss of trust between Hindus and Muslims that led to the mass exile of the former, the breakdown of the civic compact under the pressure of militants and the state—is bound to result in poetry that mourns, resists, denounces, this state of affairs. At least that is what I assumed when I began this project in summer 2008.

As I discovered very quickly, the scholarly pursuit of poetry is no more immune to the ravages of civic strife than is life itself: in two weeks in Srinagar, I could work with my collaborator for all of two days (this has been the pattern in two subsequent visits too). Strikes and curfews, public protests and police responses, ensured that no one left home unless it was absolutely necessary. I spent days indoors or on our balcony instead of in conversation with writers or aficionados of poetry, and the sounds that carried occasionally were the slogans and shouts of massed people, as well as the sharper retort of tear-gas guns and rifles. Occasionally wisps of tear gas would float past our home, located as it is on the edge of a volatile neighborhood that has long been a stronghold of the Jammu and Kashmir Liberation Front (one of several political groups allied under the banner of the Hurriyat Conference, which now leads the movement for political self-determination). The musicality, formal cadences, and intelligence of poetry seemed very far away, replaced by the muscular and polarized noise of a violence-torn public sphere. It was fitting then that one of the first arresting poems I read, brought to me in manuscript by a friend, resembled neither of the forms that are the staple of Kashmiri poetry, the *ghazal* and the *nazm*. This is (in my translation) what I read:

I am bundling the winds
I am making the night the day, day the night
I die slowly, steadily, and continue to live on
I see the desert and pull on the desert
From my eyes, oh, a river flows

I wouldn't care if they killed me
Dead, beaten, they keep me alive
I will come out of here, emerge with renewed resolve

What will they do to me, these rods and hammers?
I have, like a tear, dropped
Does a tear ever return

All that I have seen, don't ask me, oh
Those adored ones, whose flesh was burned by them
How many did not find graveyards or burial
How many were burnt on snow-mountains

How do I forget all this
What will their money and adornments do for me

I have sworn oaths on the forests
I have made to gardens this promise
I will keep watering the spring

Let them make a dog of me in prison
Once I am outside I will become a lion again
Inside, for them, I am but a lump of flesh

We will call this poet Muzaffar "Kashmiri." I learned that he had been
in prison for many years without trial, and that he was a *tehreeki* who had
taken to guns and bombs in pursuit of the dream of azadi. He was educated, but no poet—he began to write in prison, and his untitled poem
is written in a conversational (rather than literary) idiom. Its immediacy
is the product of everyday speech, of a felt urgency, and its certainties
are arrived at despairingly, in the face of imprisonment and torture. The
poem's contrasts are derived from the representations of nature that are
the staple of Kashmiri poetry: the valley is a garden, spring breezes bring
life and color, forest canopies dress the high mountains; the desert is
the life-denying polar opposite of all that constitutes Kashmiri lives
lived in harmony with nature. But in this poem the incarcerated poet
knows only paradox—he loses the distinction between day and night,
makes the desert his own, draws it around himself like a covering, lives
on even when his torturers make death attractive. What follows is the
hope brought alive in the act of the poem, the articulation of a further
resolve, the refusal to let "rods and hammers" break his will, and all this
condensed into a delicate image of no return, the tear that drops and
never climbs back.

Hope behind bars: this is the irony that anchors renewed determination in the fragility, evanescence, and finality of a shed tear. It is important though that the shed tear is not for himself, but part of a collective mourning for all those comrades, the "adored ones," whose flesh was burnt "by them" and who now lie, without proper obsequies, somewhere in the snowy mountains. Their memory, and their sacrifice, is the more certain ground of commitment that allows him to resist the promises and bribes offered by his captors (again, the unnamed "them"). In the next lines, Kashmir itself, or rather, images and tropes conventional to its poetic self-representation, provide the continuity of memory and commitment necessary for sustained faith in a political ideal:

I have sworn oaths on the forests
I have made to gardens this promise
I will keep watering the spring

The idealism of these lines veers into cliché, but the closing lines arrest that movement in an idiom, and a reality, stark and brutal:

Let them make a dog of me in prison
Once I am outside I will become a lion again
Inside, for them, I am but a lump of flesh

Both this incarcerated body, beaten into a "lump of flesh," and the unextinguished hope of release and redemption into renewed political activism ("I will become a lion again"), offer a powerful challenge to the political agents and theorists of Indian nationalism in the twenty-first century. Condensed into these last three lines is the egregious and dehumanizing practice of state power, in which the unwilling "citizen," especially one who takes to arms, is captured, tortured, and in this process, reduced to the brutalized materiality of a lump of flesh. Not everyone in Kashmir is a violent *tehreeki*, far from it, but there will be few Kashmiris who will not sympathize with the scenario and the sentiment explored by this poem. To that extent, it is representative of the collective experience of a people subject to long-drawn out and often indiscriminate state violence.

The challenge for a critic who reads poetry while thinking about politics, or indeed who reads politics via poetry, is to detail the mediations that link text and context, writing and history. There is a further difficulty: since one important definition of trauma is individual experience that cannot be properly remembered or narrated, but only reenacted in different registers of word and action, the relation between traumatic events and the practice of poetry is even more intricate.[3] The creative process that produces a poem taps into psychic mechanisms and cultural tropes (the conventional practice of a particular form of poetry, for instance) that bridges the gap between trauma as experienced by an individual and trauma as it is shared within a community. A poem is thus not a reenactment of trauma; rather, it can be thought of as a "managing" or "working through" of trauma by articulating elements of it into speech, and thus into public conversation and the record of history.[4]

However, the formal construction, the symmetries and finish, of a poem should not encourage us to believe that it is a full revelation or accounting of trauma; rather, poems can offer readers the opportunity to trace lineaments of pain and to sense the heft of all that is never quite realized or said. Indeed the form of a poem can itself be seen as a mechanism—a mode of aesthetic control—that allows the enunciation of the intense affects of trauma. For this reason alone, a poem can be a guide to what we might think of as the "phenomenology of pain" that marks conflict zones. This is even the case when the poem does not invoke events or specify histories, but is suffused with heightened emotions that are manifestly the products of civic turmoil.

Further, as poems are read, quoted, or sung in public they contribute to the collective vocabulary by which trauma is known and shared. In this, such poems and songs play a role in the formation of what Lawrence J. Kirmayer describes as a "culturally constructed landscape of memory" (1996: 175).[5] Their affective power allows them to intensify into visibility, but also to interrogate, the costs and consequences of both political mobilization and repression, whether by state agencies or those ranged against state power. Precisely because poetry draws upon and innovates within the collective resources of culture and language, the analysis of a poem can produce a more "materialist" account of political life than that offered by political scientists or even political economists who chose to sideline the affective dimensions of individual subjectivity or collective consciousness.[6]

Observers of Kashmiri lives over the last two decades have noted the fact that, as Robert Nickelsberg observes, "Indian-ruled Kashmir has one of the highest rates of post traumatic stress disorder in the world."[7] There is no question that these high levels of trauma are the product of protracted periods of political violence and oppression, and the resultant sundering of community ties and kinship networks. (This is true not only of Kashmiris in Kashmir, but also of Kashmiris who have been forced by the threat of violence to live elsewhere.) Psychiatrists and local healers have dealt with unprecedented numbers of people who exhibit recognizable symptoms of trauma; given these numbers, it is possible to argue that all aspects of Kashmiri society, culture, and politics have been reconfigured in this period by such shared suffering.[8] Further, as I will argue, such experiences have become an important basis for collective self-recognition, which means that trauma is to be understood not simply as the psychic condition of victimage, but as crucial to political mobilization. And not just trauma, but also mourning: the processions that have become central to practices of community mourning often take the form of demonstrations that combine celebrations of present and past martyrs with demands for justice and pledges to bring about the political future, the azadi, in whose name they died.[9]

In a time of such disorientation, literary writing is a powerful indicator of the way social transitions and traumas are lived by individuals and communities. Its affective range encompasses both the raw immediacy of testimonials of victims and witnesses of brutal events, and the more mediated, longer-term, reflections that they precipitate.[10] In particular, the formal structures of literary writing often enable the staging of intense human experiences that are outside the rhetorical norms of other forms of reportage. We will see, for instance, how the couplet form and the verbal repetitions of the ghazal provide a framework for observations of social suffering and disintegration that might otherwise seem disjointed or even psychotic. Stories and poems can encode insights into psychic processes that sociological observations tend to ignore; further, by exploring the links between subjective processes and public events, these texts provide insights not only into individual subjectivities but also into the making of communities (of feelings, of shared experiences, of political affiliations). While literary writing does not represent "reality" in any unmediated or uncomplicated sense, it draws upon and reworks the complexities and contradictions of human experience in ways that enable historical insights not easily available elsewhere.[11]

Theorists of trauma, particularly those who have analyzed archives of testimonials, have confronted parallel critical questions, and in this chapter I will touch upon some of the insights provided by them into the difficult links between trauma, history, and politics. There are of course many—and competing—definitions of trauma, and as many, if not more, definitions of appropriate diagnostic procedures and legitimate therapeutic methods. It is therefore necessary to state that in what follows I draw upon the work of trauma theorists not to enter into the debates that define the field, but to illuminate some of the methodological challenges that confront a critic who engages with the cultural productivity of conflict zones, and in particular, those that complicate the analysis of poems written about social suffering. As we will see, these poems render trauma not as individual loss but as social suffering: the experiences they meditate upon are not "principally psychological or medical and, therefore, *individual*," but always understood as "interpersonal" and "social."[12]

Further, even as these poems portray collective experience, they also evince the dislocation of time and refashioning of historical understanding that subtends political subjectivity. As Didier Fassin and Richard Rechtman have observed, for people who live in conflict zones, "trauma has come to give a new meaning to [the] experience of time." Continuing suffering redefines the historical understanding of those who articulate (in testimonials or in literary writing) such travails. Thus, to pay attention to the traumatic experiences of oppressed people offers insights into more than their suffering; indeed analysts can learn to produce fuller and more ethically compelling accounts of the ways in which states and elites wield power. While all studies of trauma feature the "victim," Fassin and Rechtman suggest a broader focus when they argue that to think about systemic violence in terms of its long-term traumatic effects leads to a sharper, inescapably political sense of the social world, of civic morality, and of demands for justice or reparation (2009: 275–76).

In the rest of this chapter, I will examine two poems, both ghazals, to see if they allow us to trace the process by which the articulation of trauma in an entirely conventional form of poetry bridges the gap between the disintegrated images and syntax symptomatic of individual trauma and the more orderly, consensual performance of language that is the basis of community. There exist poems whose jagged metrics and unsettled lineation perform the verbal dissociations of traumatized subjects, of language estranged from the self, but is trauma even a useful critical term when it comes to the analysis of a poetic form like the ghazal, which is a disciplined, formally self-conscious exercise in social communication? If the concerns of a ghazal, its themes and observations, call attention to an unsettled, alienating world, then what is the relationship between such insecurity and the stabilizing repetitions of the couplet form, and of the refrain, of the ghazal? The ghazal, in Kashmir and elsewhere, is an extremely well-known poetic form—then what effects does a song of social ruptures produce while it maintains the familiar conventions of the form? These are some of the methodological questions that I will explore as I think about the political affects of each poem.

POETRY AND THE LANDSCAPE OF MEMORY

Blood drips from hands, what's to me?
Bit by bit the body burns, what's to me?

Slowly, slowly it walks, where might it reach?
The sun is meandering lost on paths, what's to me?

Who, tell me, made grafts of these thorns?
So the gardens do not flower, what's to me?

Lips quiver to speak thoughts, *matyov* (o crazed one)
Tears flow from boulders, what's to me?

The mirror weeps and weeps, and watches![13]
The eyes are flooding, what's to me?

Our own become strangers sometime
Flesh pulls off nails,[14] what's to me?

The tongue stutters, the chest heaves
The meanings of words shift, what's to me?

Adam is dying, what does he observe?[15]
Massarat[16] plays with sorrows, what's to me?

Mohiuddin 'Massarat,' "Ghazal"

This poem is not only *about* traumatic events; its idiom, its choice of poetic alter ego, its inability to make connections between event and feeling, all enact the effects of trauma.[17] The poem is spoken in the voice of the *mot*, the village lunatic and seer, whose muttering or pronouncements question various forms of cultural consensus and behavior.[18] The *mot* is often depicted as wandering around and noting much in the world but then trailing off with some version of "so what do I care"?[19] "The crazed one" becomes the spokesman for this alienated world—we learn nothing of the causes of such trauma, only of its lingering, destructive effects. And yet poems like this are revelatory not only of the stresses that define Kashmiri society as it suffered (and resisted) the violence of militarized conflict but also of the intrusive, humiliating operations of the security state that became the norm after 1989. The trauma articulated in such a poem allows us to engage with the social and political consequences of long-term violence; the poem becomes a testimonial not only to emotional suffering but, as I will argue, to the political subjectivities that grow out of community responses to such sustained, profound distress.

Even when a poem speaks in the voice of an individual, it limns the contours of communities reconfigured by trauma. The solipsistic disavowal of the *mot* in Massarat's ghazal ("what's to me?") turns, as we read the poem, into an invitation to the larger theater of community suffering. In that, the poem enables an inescapably *political* understanding of the collective subjectivities that are forged in extended conflict, where entire communities come to be defined by similar experiences of brutalization. Poems like these draw upon, and in turn make available in more memorable form, the conversational idiom of the language; in this manner, poets are cultivators and curators of public memory. "What's to me," the *mot* mutters over and over again as he looks about him and lists enormities of suffering and loss; all that he notes crystallizes commonalities of feeling within, and also without, the poem. The *mot*, and the poem, joins the ordinary conversation of Kashmiris who recount experiences of vulnerability, powerlessness, and fear.[20] In each case we encounter performances of language that move the listener into empathy and perhaps understanding. This then is the poetics of trauma that informs both the work of the poet and the testimonial of the victim.

But there are analytical connections to be made before we can make the case that the affective power of such a poetics of trauma enhances our understanding of the sociohistorical situation that obtains in Kashmir. After all, such poems (and many other texts of trauma) do not provide easy evidence for the generation of facile political claims. Massarat's "Ghazal," for example, offers little that translates into a politics; its tone and concerns are far from those associated with political activism or any form of resistance politics. In fact its power lies in its amplified performance of the broken self and community, in its enactment of a loss and betrayal so profound that the poem spirals into the vertigo of traumatized subjectivity. Even as the *mot* registers loss and misery around him, his is a solipsistic disavowal of fellow feeling, a retreat into agonized separation.[21] Is there then any recovery from the agon of the *mot*, and of the poem?

One answer lies in the form of the ghazal, in which each semi-autonomous couplet creates the logic of the whole. In this ghazal, each couplet counterpoints the despair of the *mot* with a series of images that offer a context for his disassociation: he observes bleeding hands, burning bodies, lost pathways, grafts of thorns, blighted gardens, quivering lips that do not speak, in short, a world under siege. His muttered refusal to feel, his turning away ("what's to me?") is juxtaposed against all that he catalogues so vividly; his seeming indifference is a failing attempt to distance the surreal images of violence that fragment his world. Images from a nightmare (weeping rocks and mirrors) bleed into suggestions of torture (skin peeling off nails, muted tongues, broken backs). This is a world of strangers, "our own" now alienated from each other.

Language itself is disoriented—the phrase "the meanings of words shift" could be a description of the linguistic symptoms of trauma—but the couplet form of the ghazal holds steady, creating structure and control. When we get to the self-reflexive closing couplet (the *makta*), which conventionally calls attention to the poet and thus to the craft of poetry, the *mot*, the disassociated voice of the poem, is set against "Massarat," the poet whose craft "plays with troubles." Here, the *mot* is the overwrought alter ego of the poet, for only a crazed one can speak of the intensities of disorder and grief that mark the death of mankind ("*Adam*").[22] In this ghazal then, in the internal dynamic between the voice of the *mot* and the craft of the poet, that is, in the contrast between the idiom and affects of social trauma and a formal regularity and structure, the poem enacts not a turning away from the world but a more powerful illumination of its condition.

These poetic intensities of feeling are, after all, the affective glue that binds readers into community (even as they read about, and perhaps identify with, the destruction of community).[23] This is also a community forged in language; that is, this is a ghazal whose idiom is that of conversational Kashmiri, and the poem intensifies the everyday register of language. The *mot* speaks in the vernacular, with little of the "elevated" diction and self-consciously poetic phraseology that often mars the ghazal, and his voice is that of his community. Thus, in the social matrix of the poem, in the continuity between its imagined and historical community, what might seem to be a poetics of victimage, a restating of enervating loss alone, enables, in reading, retelling, and sharing, both the recognition, and the confirmation, of community.

Perhaps even more important, such affective identification—"yes, we know this feeling"—is also an important step in the realization of the resistance politics of survivors, people who understand themselves as living at the mercy of arbitrary power, but also as people committed to restoring their sense of self and confirming their ideal of self-determined futures. In commonality of suffering, and the shared idiom of testimonial and poetry, lie the roots of strengthened political community. If the *mot* performs the traumatized subject, the poet redefines that trauma, shapes it into the text of communal grief. This is no easy or natural process, for thinking with and through such poetry, or indeed such testimony, makes great demands on readers and listeners (as well academic critics): to enter this world is to be moved to a respectful engagement with the experiences of those who have suffered violence. It is also to learn how powerfully those experiences help feed a politics of resistance.

That is, literary texts offer readers not only a strong realization of the effects of violence and trauma, but also make more pointed the sense (in Caruth's words): "that history, like trauma, is never simply one's own, that history is precisely the way we are implicated in each other's traumas" (1996: 24). To write on texts that manifest collective suffering is to become caught up in that history, to articulate oneself into the communities shaped by shared experiences of, and then memories of, violence and dislocation. This is not only a matter of willed empathy, or the choice to identify with those whose lives were and continue to be molded by political and military aggression. Rather, it is a forceful recognition that the stuttering uncertainties of fear, mourning, alienation, and rage, or indeed the backward-looking melancholia, that characterize such writing make demands on everything from the modes of analysis deployed by commentators to (more occasionally) the stylistic features of their prose. These are unexpected complications to be sure, but they also lead to hopeful communication: that is the promise of reading attentively the traumatic effects of sustained conflict. The first and crucial step in the analyst's or cultural critic's task is to re-affirm as empathetically as possible the recurrent crises that are experienced by those at the receiving end of the exercise of power. Such empathy, as I have suggested above, also lends analytical insight into collectivities that are reshaped by shared experiences of suffering as well as enables a recognition of the power of such experiences to shape any imagined future.[24]

"EXPERIENCE" AND THE POLITICS OF
NATION FORMATION

For Indian policy planners, politicians, and citizens, the fact that for over two decades Kashmiris have suffered extraordinary military and civil violence is simply to be understood as the unfortunate but unavoidable consequence of a violent secessionist politics. Conversely, for Kashmiri proponents of azadi, it is precisely such experiences that confirm their alienation from an Indian nation whose security forces have long brutalized them. The experiences of ordinary Kashmiris—and no one has remained untouched by such violence—are to them crucial to the case they make for the legitimacy of Kashmiri self-determination, and both activists and sympathetic scholars insist that there is no "moving on" from this horrific record. On the other hand, nationalist policy makers hold that those civil rights groups, political activists, and scholars who concentrate on the history of such violence in order to argue for the legitimacy of Kashmiri self-determination marginalize the fact that large numbers of Kashmiris have joined or voted for pro-India political parties, and that these parties have been democratically elected to power in repeated state elections.[25]

In recent years then, "experience"—in particular the experience of trauma—has become important to the debate about the present and future of Kashmiri politics. Civil society activists and human rights lawyers continue to document individual and community suffering as part of their demands for justice and civic restitution. They call for punishment for all who are violent, including those who torture, kill and maim in the name of national security. For them, the troubling unknowns of traumatic events need to be brought into legal view: the law has the resources to recognize, intervene into, and offer judgments that will be therapeutic. Further, such accounting is necessary to understand why functionaries and institutions of the state are so quick to give up on their commitment to democratic functioning. For Indian nationalists who sympathize with the suffering of Kashmiris (but who oppose the idea of a separate Kashmiri nation) the heft and burden of traumatic experience must be acknowledged in order to be mourned and set aside in the interest of a peaceful nationalized future. For votaries of Kashmiri independence, there is no question of forgetting—all such experiences must be memorialized and thus activated further, for they fuel a resurgent movement for freedom.

In this context, Massarat's ghazal is an eloquent witness to its distressed world, a powerful expression of the miseries and struggles that came to define Kashmir. As I said before, the poem states no causes for the social and personal disintegration it charts, but the tortured voice of the *mot* joins the many Kashmiri voices that have since testified to their vulnerability and suffering during these two decades. As this short poem knows, prolonged trauma renders the world threatening and shifting, and alliances seem as fragile as they may have been life-saving ("Our own become strangers sometime"). Bodies are broken ("Flesh pulls off nails"), words lose their meanings, mankind—*Adam*—lies dying. Of the many anxious questions that seem to motivate the poem, the most troubling asks about the nature of survival: will we ever be as we were once, or is that world lost entirely? In which case, who are *we* who must live in this alienated, inhospitable world?

Ironically, the precariousness of the world of the poem is a poignant reminder that the destruction and disintegration it witnesses have become conditions of political being in Kashmir. As people renew daily routines after periods of intense violence and civic restriction, they learn that *resistance* is not only an activist mode embodied in those who join the armed *tehreek*, or even those who throw stones, but is also asserted by those who simply go about their lives. Even in periods of political turmoil, including while under curfew, people find ways to procure food and medicine, to

share information, and, occasionally, to take to the streets. This is the re-
silience of the everyday, and it adds up to a massive and courageous refusal
to let the state of militarized occupation define every aspect of life. One
way to be revenged on the brutality of the actions of people in authority
is to survive their worst efforts, to go back home, to return to threatened
patterns of everyday life, and thus to refuse to let official imperatives and
actions, arrogance and paranoia, define individual and community.[26] This
is by no means easy, and sometimes impossible; and even when a precarious normality is achieved, little that is destructive is forgotten, and rarely
forgiven.

LOOKING HOMEWARD: POETRY AND/AS DISPLACEMENT

The narrative of Kashmiri suffering and resistance offered here, and of the
witness of poetry, folds within itself another particularly poignant story,
that of the mass exit of Kashmiri Pandits in the winter of 1989–90 and
in the years that followed. Two decades later, few have moved back to
Kashmir to live there, though large numbers visit, especially to congre-
gate at their age-old temples on days of religious significance. While there
are perhaps four thousand Pandits who continue to live in Kashmir, the
vast majority are estranged from their homeland and from their neighbors, and see themselves as living in exile. As their lives, and those of their
children, take root in places outside of Kashmir, the possibility of return
becomes ever more remote. Many voice their sense of betrayal and anger,
but also the hope, however fading, of return and reconciliation.[27]

Kashmiri Pandit poets, even in the early years of their displacement,
wrote of seemingly insurmountable distances, and of their longing for
their homes and for the lives they shared with their Muslim neighbors.
Poets mourned the loss of their homes, but also sustained hopes of restored
lives, and a revival of the composite culture that sustained them.[28] In the
poem that follows, written no more than three years after the first large
groups of Pandits left Kashmir, Brij Nath "Betaab" yearns for a life now
lost, and closes with a promise of return and reunion.[29] Betaab's ghazal
takes the form of a series of questions addressed to his Muslim friend and
fellow poet, Afaq Aziz, all asking if everyday life in their village is the same
as it was before the Pandits left. It ends with a pledge to resume ties and
family friendship beyond the present estrangement—but only once Aziz

says that "normal" life has been resumed. Betaab's poem is at once deeply conventional in its imagination of Kashmir as a pastoral landscape where lives are lived in harmony with nature and with neighbors, and profoundly unconventional in that it struggles with the unimaginable and traumatic breach that is the contemporary exile of the Pandits of Kashmir.

The passage of time is a major theme in this poem too, time refracted, rendered disjointed by crisis. As we will see, the poem is profoundly nostalgic about the home that once was (so much so that that home seems an imagined idyll). However, it is also powerfully aware that change is visible everywhere, as villages take on the attributes of towns and small towns expand. The pastoral form of Kashmir, the mode in which it was long imagined, retreats into the past as life is transformed by the expansion of markets and the growth of a cash-centered economy. Ironically, for the displaced Pandits, these changes in the villages and cities they lived in compound and, worse, disguise, the enormous breach in personal and community history that they know in their exile. The hometowns and villages they left behind are increasingly built-up, modernized, even prosperous; none of these processes seem affected by or even cognizant of their absence, their exile. Once vital to the Kashmiri body, they are now missing, but life still pulses, in some ways more robustly than in the past. This then is the question that haunts the poem and has haunted the community ever since: for Pandits, everything has changed, but has anyone at home, caught up in the twin compulsions of the conflict and the coming of consumer culture, even noticed?

Ah! Will not the flower bloom in the garden as in the past?
Does the bulbul perch on the window-sill to sing, as in the past?

Have our village gardens been turned into market gardens yet?
Does no one ask for a basketful of greens, as in the past?

Do the village children still gather at the milkman's store?
Do they still invent nicknames—sparrowhawk—as in the past?

Does anyone come asking neighbours for *gurus*?
Does anyone bring the cow a *dul*, as in the past?

Does daughter-in-law still bring birth-gifts from her mother's house?
Does the carpenter craft—anywhere?—a cradle, as in the past?

Is grain still dried on plain straw-mats?
Is the pestle-and-mortar found anywhere, as in the past?

Are mud-walls felled the same way even today?
Do children eat mulberry in hiding, as in the past?

Does anyone sing and dance on the Vyeth's banks on Eid?
Does anyone boat down to Tulla-Mulla, as in the past?

How much are we going to taunt each other?
Do you think we'll never come together, as in the past?

Betaab says he will come home when Afaq Aziz
Sends word that Sister picks up the new *longun*, as in the past.

Brij Nath "Betaab," "Ghazal"

Betaab's ghazal is a compendium of the sights and sounds, relationships and everyday practices that signified the face-to-face community life of villages in Kashmir.[30] The opening couplet sets the pastoral scene—the flowers in the garden, the intimacy of songbirds perched on window-sills. The next opposes a single discordant note, the coming of a "market-garden,"[31] to its fond melody of the commons, "the village gardens," and its correlative, the neighbor who asks for a basketful of greens, probably freshly picked from the small kitchen garden that each family cultivates. The third continues in this vein, shifting the scene to the children in the village playing together, and invoking a practice for which Kashmiris pride themselves, which is giving individuals nicknames that are then used by the community at large. These children surface later too—their carefree lives include climbing up mud walls to pilfer ripe mulberries from a tree in someone's garden (and of course mud walls crumble!). The poet lists the everyday activities of the village: feeding domesticated cattle grass from clay receptacles (*dul*), drying grain on straw mats, pounding the mortar and pestle. Several lines of the poem develop the informalities and per-sonalized relations that texture village communities: the neighbor who comes to ask for *gurus*, the news that is shared when a new mother returns bearing gifts from her natal home (she is referred to as "daughter-in-law," for that is who she is not only within her husband's family, but also within the community).

The poem's remembered idylls of the village are, of course, qualified in each couplet by the relentless, unforgiving, question: is it still so today, "as in the past?" Even as the poem revives that innocent, charmed life, it becomes clear that this life exists only in fond memory (if it did exist at all), and is now superseded. Nostalgia suffuses memory here, transforming its attempts to revive community into a rueful recognition of its passing. There is a vast, unstated chasm between the past and the present, but the poem does not, till the last three couplets, suggest any reasons for that divide. It is only then that the poem shifts away from its reverie and brings into view the sociopolitical elements of the changes that bedevil these memories. The ninth couplet asks if religious festivals, both Muslim and Hindu, are celebrated as they were in the past, and the answer—if only in its painful silence—is clear: Muslims might still sing the joy of *Eid* on the banks of the Jhelum, but Pandits will no longer take boats down the same river to the important Hindu shrine at Tulla-Mulla. They do not live by the banks of the *Vyeth*, the Jhelum, any more.

At this point, in the penultimate couplet, Betaab directly addresses his friend Afaq Aziz, but also, by extension, both the Muslim and Pandit communities: "How much are we going to taunt each other? / Do you think we'll never come together, as in the past?" No events are named, perhaps because to do so would be too painful and divisive; the question that lingers is simply that of the divide, and of how to overcome it in a context where the drive to affix blame overrides—at least in the moment—the desire to be reconciled and reunited. The poem closes, however, in a powerful gesture of reciprocity: the Pandit Betaab will return when his Muslim friend and neighbor Afaq Aziz tells him that his wife (who the poet calls "Sister" in the poem) has resumed the generosity that once marked the shared lives of Muslims and Hindus in Kashmir. She will once again wield the *longun* with which she once measured rice to cook for all those who visit, and Betaab will know that he is welcome and at home. As in the earlier couplets of the poem, the signifier of restored lives is an everyday object in the kitchen, the very ordinariness, the domesticity, of the *longun*, a marker of the humanity that will resist and outlive political divides and conflicts. And yet, for all that it is a marker of hope, the archaism of the *longun* (an object now no longer to be found in most Kashmiri kitchens) lingers and challenges—if the object, and the term, are so thoroughly of the past, can it, will it, ever indicate a renewed future?

Given the divergent experiences that motivate each ghazal, their concerns and vocabulary are quite distinct. However, both poems are born out of the same conflict zone, and each produces a vivid picture of personal and community trauma. In both cases, violence—the origin of trauma and social suffering—is not identifiable as or reducible to a singular event. But it is everywhere and its effects are profound as it tears apart communities and remolds individual and communal subjectivities.[32] To let these poems lead us to an understanding of trauma is to have that term expand beyond the heightened and troubled affect or psychological disorientation of an individual to a more encompassing sense of community history. In a parallel instance, Saiba Varma describes Kashmiri patients at a psychiatric clinic refusing to "locate their suffering within a specific catastrophic event." She reports that they "preferred to speak of their daily struggles of life under occupation: how they worried about the safety of their children when they went to school, how it was impossible to be healthy in Kashmir, and how their quality of life or livelihoods had suffered because of frequent strikes and shutdowns" (2013). These poems, I have argued, enact similar traumatic histories.

Even as each poet crafts a formally structured and conventional response to an "impossible history," it is clear that the poem seethes with energies, emotions, experiences it cannot "entirely possess" or contain. The tension between the symmetry of couplets and controlled repetitions of the ghazal and the dislocations and broken lives that are their theme suggest the pulse of life in conflict zones, the struggle to achieve "normality" in the face of extraordinary experiences that tear apart lives and everyday routines. Poems that feature this precarious dynamic between the centripetal logic of poetic form and the centrifugal thrust of the vocabulary and imagery of civic disintegration and displacement indicate why, in zones of conflict, poetry takes on an affective force that it need not possess in less charged and burdened contexts. The particularity and power of such poems—of the poetics of trauma more broadly—is that they move their readers not simply into fellow-feeling (the "yes, I know this emotion" moment) but cause them to know the more disturbing demands of political empathy within and across communitarian divides.

Which is not to say that Kashmiri readers of these poems (or indeed readers elsewhere) will come to the same political analysis or understanding. That hope is utopian, and perhaps facile, given the situation that exists in Kashmir. At first reading, Mohiuddin Massarat's ghazal speaks for Kashmiri Muslims in Kashmir who see themselves at the receiving end of the undemocratic practices of Indian institutions and as targeted, not protected, by the security establishment. In similar vein, Brij Nath Betaab's ghazal articulates the loss known by Kashmiri Hindus who have moved away from Kashmir and who see themselves as victims of armed militants and their sympathizers among the majority community. These separate resentments—and, for all their polarized differences, these parallel modes of suffering—mark the troubled lives of Kashmiris today. These are also the ill feelings and the anger that fuel their survival, their political positions and practices, and their dreams of different futures.

Poems, like other forms of performance, can be mobilized to serve very different political ends; there are those who will read each poem as testimony of forms of suffering that are not shared by Kashmiris but are in fact exclusive to one community or the other. Narrations of the traumatic past can of course be shaped to generate not greater openness and mutuality but to cement exclusionary identities. It is, however, my argument that these poems themselves refuse such exclusions. They do so precisely because they speak powerfully to their moment and preserve it, not as inert or past, but as the living precursor of ours, and as a necessary, living component of the future. Massarat's *mot* is not marked as either Muslim or Hindu, and elements of the social suffering he articulates have scarred the lives of all Kashmiris. Similarly, even as Betaab's poem speaks of Pandit dislocation and exile, it is addressed to his Muslim friend Afaq Aziz and mourns the loss of togetherness and hopes for a revival of shared lives. I have argued here that even as we pay careful attention to these poems, to their specificities and their differences, we should do so—and the poems demand this—in a fashion that returns their representations of trauma and lost lives to collective histories. If these shared histories contain stories of divergent dispossession and suffering, they also contain in them memories, and indeed the very *language*, with which to imagine futures different from, and more humane and equitable than, those pasts and indeed our present.

1. Ironically, a commentator unsympathetic to Kashmiri self-determination has most precisely recognized that its present mobilization derives great force from shared suffering over the last two decades. In April 2012, Manu Joseph infamously parodied political anger in Kashmir by styling it a "heritage" industry:

> Trauma in Kashmir is like a heritage building—the elite fight to preserve it. "Don't forget," is their predominant message. "Don't forget to be traumatised." They want the wound of Kashmir to endure because the wound is what indicts India for the many atrocities of its military. This might be a long period of calm, but if the wound vanishes, where is the justice? India simply gets away with all those rapes, murders and disappearances? So nothing disgusts them more than these words: "Normalcy returns to Kashmir"; "Peace returns to the Valley"; "Kashmiris want to move on." (Joseph 2012)

For Joseph, trauma, like a second skin, can be sloughed off when the time is right. The poems I analyze here suggest otherwise.

2. Jayalal Kaul shows that Lal Děd, for instance, adapted and modified Sanskritic forms of words into modern Kashmiri, and crafted from them an idiom still in use. His examples are: "*loh-langar* (iron anchor) for involvement in worldly things; *seki lavar vuthu'ny* (twisting a rope of sand) for a fruitless occupation; *vatanā'sh* (highway robbers) for greed, lust and pride; *sandā'rith pakhu'c* (steadying the wheels) for equipoise; *da'ly trāvu'ny* (spreading the hem of the garment) for surrender and supplication; *dumatas rinzy* (marbles thrown at a huge boulder) for an ineffective attempt, and many more. . . . This is so also with the imagery drawn naturally from the familiar surroundings of the countryside: the ferry across the river, the creaky bridges on the causeway, the bloom of a cotton flower, the kailyard, the saffron field . . . etc. etc." (J. Kaul 1973: 65–66).

3. This is not to suggest that communities cannot experience trauma—they can and do. In fact, belonging to a community can both intensify, and help come to terms with, an individual's trauma. The links between individual and community experiences of, and responses to, trauma are often best made visible in cultural artifacts, particularly those whose reiteration becomes an index of the affective energies and political energies circulating within the community.

4. In that, poems do similar psychological work, and serve similar cultural and memorial functions, as do testimonies of those who suffer trauma. The narrative forms of testimonials are important to their meaning and affect too, but since poetry foregrounds form, it seems to work at a greater remove from experience than does any form of testimonial.

5. Kirmayer also offers a useful definition of the way in which traumatic experiences, in their reiteration and sharing, become cultural memory: "Landscapes of memory are given shape by the personal and social significance of specific memories but also draw from *meta-memory*—implicit models of memory which influence what can be recalled and cited as veridical. Narratives of trauma may be understood then as cultural constructions of personal and historical memory" (175).

6. Scholars who write about state formation, governance, and international relations rarely distinguish their vocabulary from that deployed by policy makers and administrators (this is of course the primary way in which they hope to influence the operations of state power). The historiography that results is inevitably a legitimation of the priority of the state in the making of human histories. This is the historiography of what *is*, of analyses that are limited by a "realist" recognition that the crucial question is that of power: Do agents of the state have the resources to mold the political aspirations of people to suit their idea of the nation, or not? How coercive must the state apparatus be in order to preserve the "nation," which is, after all, the unitary ideal in whose service this apparatus is supposedly constructed?

7. See Nikelsberg 2008, Amin and Khan 2009, de Jong et al. 2008 and a great many other websites. See also Human Rights Watch 2006. Wani 2013, reports on the connection between torture and sexual trauma.

8. Saiba Varma is developing an important body of work on these issues; see for instance, Varma 2012. The language of personal and community trauma is widely spoken in Kashmir. Manisha Gangahar quotes Amit Wanchoo as saying "Each one of us has been a part of a tragedy that can offer no catharsis" (2013: 42). In recounting many fearful encounters with army soldiers, Dr M. Ashraf Bhat writes: "This is just one of the many incidents which happened with us: some could save their lives and many could not. This and many such haunting stories are still occupying my mental space and I genuinely don't understand how to deal with them. It is indeed paranoiac. Since then, every time I see an army man, I recall the nightmare, I fear the same treatment" (2014).

9. See for instance Adil Lateef's news report on a funeral gathering and procession (2013).

10. In areas of conflict, literary writers are of course not the only ones to focus on the powerful social and political role played by suffering and heightened feelings. Journalists who report on the many killings, public protests, and official reprisals often quote victims, or families of victims, who testify to the culture of fear and insecurity that mars their lives. Anthropologists and other scholars, particularly those studying the rise in mental diseases, also record the miseries of individuals and their families. Political analysts too take note of periods of intense public anger—as when, in 2010, young boys (*sangbaaz* or stone-pelters) engaged the police in unequal battles, and over a hundred of them were killed—but only long enough to suggest that such heightened emotions, while weighty in the moment, will eddy away in the face of other political developments.

11. In a parallel argument, Françoise Davoine and Jean-Max Gaudillière argue that poetry, like fiction from war zones, should be understood as "neither an ornament nor a cultural product: it is a necessary instrument of historicization" (2004: 116).

12. These terms and distinctions are articulated by the editors in the "Introduction" to their landmark volume *Social Suffering* (Kleinman et al. 1998: ix).

13. The syntax of the original line can also suggest a person weeping and watching (himself) in the mirror. This line thus links the "tears" of inanimate objects like boulders or mirrors to human eyes that flood with tears.

14. In Kashmiri, *nam te maaz* (nails and flesh) is an idiomatic phrase used to suggest closeness—between brother and sister for instance, or the closest of friends. Here, following upon the previous line, "Our own become strangers," the literalization of this metaphor (flesh pulled off nails) suggests torture, which brutalizes not only the individual body but also tears apart the family, the community.

15. *Adam* here is mankind; his dying the death of all.

16. *Massarat*, the poet's *takhallus* (pen-name) means happiness, here in contrast with the "sorrows" with which he "plays."

17. *Sheereza*, (Kashmiri) 38: 3–5 (2006), 198.

18. For a story that captures the cultural significance and vatic power of the *mot*, see Parrey 2011.

19. This phrase also signals the strategic passivity that is a response to existential crisis—in Kashmir, as in other conflict zones, survival often demands such distancing. Also, "what's to me" (*me kyah*) suggests the ironic tone of the jester who notes and calls attention to what is untoward, only to disavow what he sees and hears. The wicked ironies of the *mot*'s observations are to be found in contemporary humor too, as when a Kashmiri protestor, threatened by a policeman who has heard him join a crowd in shouting "Indian dogs go away," insists that he has in fact been saying, *sotto voce*, "Indian dogs stay here."

20. See for instance the testimonials recorded in the report *Alleged Perpetrators* (International Tribunal for Human Rights and Justice in Indian Administered Kashmir and the Association of Parents of Disappeared Persons 2012) and by Shobhna Sonpar (2007).

21. This isolation reminds us of the power of Cathy Caruth's question, "Is the trauma the encounter with death, or the ongoing experience of having survived it?" (1996: 7).

22. Agha Shahid Ali writes that the "ghazal is not an occasion for angst; it is an occasion for genuine grief." (2000: 13).

23. Sara Ahmed writes that one of the effects of writing that deploys intense emotions is "to mediate the relationship between the psychic and the social, and between the individual and collective." "Emotions *do things*," she states, "and they align individuals with communities" (119). In her argument, "affective economies" should be understood as producing not only "psychic" but also "social and material" conditions (121); that is, the textual circulation of intense emotions has material consequences, marking out particular bodies and defining communities (2004).

24. Dominick LaCapra argues for the value of the "empathetic unsettlement" that is produced in the work of the "attentive secondary witness" (the poet, the literary critic, the historian) of historical trauma (78). He suggests that for historians who write on experiences of trauma, "empathy is a counterforce to victimization," and plays an important role "both in historical understanding and in the ethics of everyday life." For him, "the role of empathy" is to allow connections to be made between "historical understanding, social critique, and ethico-political activity," that is, the exercise of empathy enables critical theory to be better related to political practice

(2001: 219). LaCapra's ideas are extended forcefully in Michael Rothberg's insistence that "Trauma theory helps make us attentive to suffering and thus, in principle, to justice and responsibility, but it needs to be supplemented by a positive vision of social and political transformation" (2003: 156).

25. There has been an increase in voter turnout in recent elections, particularly in state Assembly elections, in spite of calls for election boycotts. Analysts remain divided about the meaning of such high turnouts, particularly since many voters say that they participate in order to elect local administrators who will pay attention to everyday problems rather than as a vote of confidence in India.

26. In a parallel instance, Iris Jean-Klein's analysis of the lives of Palestinians during the Intifada argues that their daily activities during periods when regular life is "suspended" (by Israeli military action or by the response of the Palestinian leadership) adds up to an "everyday activism" that allows communities to "self-nationalize." That is, their daily routines, including the forms of their domesticity, at such moments follow from, renew, and shape their political awareness and commitment to the cause. Jean-Klein argues that such transformations of daily life play an important role in generating the forms of both Palestinian resistance politics and nationalist identity (2001).

27. Siddhartha Gigoo's novel *The Garden of Solitude* (2001) provides a humane account of the miseries and modes of survival of the Pandits dislocated from Kashmir in the 1990's. Mahanandju, one of the elderly characters in the novel, slips into derangement once he leaves Kashmir and is forced to live in tawdry refugee camps or cheap rented rooms: "The calendar on the wall lost its meaning. No one looked at it. . . . It was difficult for Mahanandju to tell the past from the present. He longed to live life backwards (85)." At several such moments, the narrative describes forms of alienation and disorientation that parallel those depicted in Massarat's ghazal, one mode of Kashmiri suffering mirroring another.

28. See for instance the *nazm* by Som Nath Bhat "Veer," "A New Day Will Dawn," in *Aalav* (Kashmiri), (Jammu: Department of Information, Jammu and Kashmir Government), Nov.–Dec. 2003: 40–41. The poem is reprinted in this volume.

29. "Betaab" (Brij Nath's *takhallus*) means restless or impatient or uneasy. Given the circumstances of the poet's dislocation, his pen name is apposite.

30. Original in Kashmiri. Published in Aziz 2003, 108–9.

31. This reference to the coming of market-gardens provides a glimpse into one of the extraordinary features of the conflict years in Kashmir, which is the growth of a cash economy (and in towns, a consumer culture). In that, Kashmir's cities and towns are no different from those in India, but here, the rise in standards of living and in conspicuous consumption is particularly unsettling, given that they parallel huge losses of lives, large numbers of people jailed or "disappeared," a rise in violence against women, and a larger loss of cultural coherence and confidence. On the one hand, a living history of trauma and loss, on the other, a remarkable expansion of expensive urban homes, shops and malls.

32. As Caruth has suggested, the psychic productivity of trauma—dreams and flashbacks—should be understood as rooted not only in the unconscious but also in history: "The traumatized," she writes, "carry an impossible history within them, or they become themselves the symptom of a history that they cannot entirely possess" (1995: 3–12).

Villagers run from a police charge after a funeral procession | Lesar, February 2012

A boatman on the frozen Dal Lake | Srinagar, February 2007

A woman prays inside Dastgeer Sahib in Khanyar, days after the shrine was
destroyed by a mysterious fire | Srinagar, July 2012

Villagers work in their field as a paramilitary soldier stands guard | Anantnag,
April 2013

Rashid "Kanispuri"

Ghazal

Tārkan az mālu' karu'khā kunuy zon
Tāru' gọlāb nālas jaru'khā kunuy zon

Kafnu'n tsūran hu'nz yi bạstī zāg hẏth
Pāsu' sọn yeti tsạ garkhā kunuy zon

Achu'r tsādạr hẏth natsān az śehrōgām
Dunihik gham halmas barkhā kunuy zon

Piyāhu' mōtuk con chu lạzim prẏth ạkis
Marō ạkhū'r kiā tsu' maru'khā kunuy zon

'umri hu'ndi gul sūr gạy brenzis andar
Sāth nūruk vantu' sarkhā kunuy zon

Sang gạmu't nōzuk badan yakhbastu' dil
Śīn vẏglẏkh vạẓfu' pau'khā kunuy zon

Vethi tarav khūr vāyav ạs sạmith
Kath chē ṣirātạṣ tsu' taru'khā kunuy zon

Rashid "Kanispuri"

Ghazal

Will you make a garland of the stars today, all by yourself
Will you set a rose-collar with barbed wire, all by yourself

This neighbourhood of shroud-stealers on the prowl,
Will you craft ornaments of the purest gold here, all by yourself

Swathed in tatters, wandering in cities and villages today
Will you fill your mantle with the world's sorrows, all by yourself

Everyone must drink from the cup of death
We will die in the end, will you die all by yourself

The blooms of a lifetime turned ash in a moment
Say, will you explore the auspicious moment all by yourself

Tender bodies have turned stone, hearts frozen-ice
Will you melt the snow, will you read a prayer all by yourself

We'll cross the *Vyeth*, we'll row all together
The issue is, will you cross the *Sirat*[1] all by yourself

....

Published in *Sheeraza* (Kashmiri) 38:3–5 (2006), 206.

Rashid "Kanispuri" was born in 1955 in Kanispora, Baramulla. He has a BA from Degree College, Baramulla, and an MA in psychology from Punjab University. He retired as a deputy superintendent of police. He has published volumes of poetry, and was awarded the Bal Sahitya Puraskar by the Sahitya Akademi for *Gul te Bulbul* (2013).

NOTE

1. It is said that on the Day of Judgment all must cross over *Jehannum* (Hell) on the *Pul-i-Sirat*, a hair-thin thread; sinners will find it impossible, but for the good the hair-bridge will widen.

Pyare "Hatash"

Ghazal

Rātas cham vuzu'nāvān rāth
Kanḍẏn pẏṭh sāvān rāth

    Yādan ẏeli chim kru'ạr voṭhān
    Choru'choru' cham karnāvān rāth

Guhul śihul virivāran hund
Aksar yād mẏ pāvān rāth

    Sanu' chum ạndrī man sạdras
    Vāvu' maslar tulnāvān rāth

Caśman hu'nz vạhrāth gahē
Buku' buku' cham vadu'nāvān rāth

    Koṭ tsol prōn su voṇdu'vu'śniēr
    Ti sori sori hạndrāvān rāth

Yinu' rāvī goṇmạthi naẓar
Rōz Hatāś ghazlāvān rāth

Pyare "Hatash"

Ghazal

The night stirs me up at night
On thorns I am put to sleep by the night

> When scabs on my memories peel
> I am thrashed about by the night

The deep shade of willow groves—
I'm often reminded by the night

> Distraught are the seas of my heart
> Wind-whipped waves raised by the night

Sometimes the eyes flood over
In spurts, I am made to weep by the night

> Where has it run away, that old winter's warmth
> That slowly, slowly causes the night to pass

Careful you don't lose the seer's vision
Remain, *Hatash*, singing ghazals though the night

....

Published in *Sheeraza* (Kashmiri) 31:4 (1997), 129.

Jawahir Lal "Saroor"

Ghazal

Kathi gāmu'ts kọth akhbār vuchiv
Mạti ābas tarnas tār vuchiv

    Yinu' dapu'has pholi yeti pōśu' caman
    Pod pod chu dazān az nār vuchiv

Ḍol mạnzi athan rang mahrenē
Mahrāzan vothi dastār vuchiv

    Vatu' sārē ratu' sū'ti rangu'nạvith
    Prŷth vati pŷṭh yeti śahmār vuchiv

Kartāmath yeti ōs Rāmun rāj
Zindu' rōzun az kal bār vuchiv

    Kath karmu' Sarūras vu'ni chanu' pay
    Laegh lāru'ki kartām dār vuchiv!

Jawahir Lal "Saroor"

Ghazal

Speech has gone awry, at newspapers take a look
For a way across roiled waters, take a look

> Don't say that flower gardens bloomed here
> Each footfall burns—today the flames, take a look

The henna leaches from the hands of brides
Bridegrooms' turbans knocked off, take a look

> All paths have been colored deep with blood
> On each path here a king-serpent, take a look

Sometime in the past there was Ram's rule here
Nowadays living is a burden, take a look

> Don't speak, *Saroor* does not know yet
> People are scattered here and there, take a look!

....

Published in *Aalav* (Nov.–Dec. 2003), 29.

Fayaz Tilgami

Ghazal

Vuṭh tse chī larzān kēnh bāvun chuyā
Caśmu' phiri phiri chukh vuchān rāvun chuyā

Ṭāri zan khotyī nu' yāry̐n hund śuhul
Tāp saḥrāvan andar chāvun chuyā

Lōnci manz yim yīti ǎvili khāb hy̐th
Kongi kihē aftāb bramrāvun chuyā

Brōnt kǎmisund goy tsu' kas ālav divan
Beyiti kānh ajṇabi tse azmāvun chuyā

Bạli ti mā āsakh tsu' ǎnas khay tulān
Yād beyi piōmut panun yāvun chuyā

Miạni pạ̄ṭhy̐n rōvmut āsī vajūd
Miạni pạ̄ṭhy̐n nāv badlāvun chuyā

Fayaz Tilgami

Ghazal

Your lips are trembling, have something to say, do you
Your eyes dart around, you wish to disappear, do you

So the shade of pines doesn't impress you
Wish to enjoy the desert sun, do you

Knotted into garments are these very tender dreams[1]
Like the saffron-setting sun, you wish to dwindle, do you?

Who do you seem to recognize, who do you call out to
Here too, do you wish to test some stranger, do you

You wouldn't pointlessly be removing a mirror's stains—
Remembered again your youth, have you

Like me, you must have lost your being
Like me, you wish to change your name, do you

....

Published in *Sheeraza* (Kashmiri), 38:3–5 (2006), 196.

Fayaz Tilgami was born in 1950 at Tilgam, Pattan. He completed B.Ed. and MA degrees, including an MA in Kashmiri. He retired as a Lecturer in Kashmiri. He has published literary criticism, a biography of Nishat Ansari (G. M. Ansari), essays, and a volume of poems, *Lajawab*.

NOTE

1. The word *lonchi* in the original means a knot tied into the corner of a loose garment, into which money or small valuables are folded.

Bashir "Zair"

Ghazal

Bāzar kunum me vān kunum kār tey kunum
Sōdā salaf kunum tu' khrīdār tey kunum

Sōdāg̣arī me pēśu' tavay chum kunun tagān
Dilbar kunum yi dil kunum dil dār tey kunum

Pạ̄nsuk havas yi chum tu' takhayyul girav thovum
Sōncuk yi son sodur kunum iẓhār tey kunum

Bāpār mazhabuk korum dīnas ti nŷth hetsu'm
Kạmi von faqat me lōl kunum yār tey kunum

Kyā kyā kunum tu' kas kunum sōruy magar kunum
Prath vaqtu' panun pān kyā kirdār tey kunum

Insān dạpith insạniyat rūdus masakh karān
Zāir buthiuk me mạrimond anhār tey kunum

Bashir "Zair"

Ghazal

The market I sold, the shop I sold, work too I sold
Goods and things I sold, the customer too I sold

> Trade is my profession that's why I know how to sell
> My beloved I sold, this heart I sold, my lover too I sold

So greedy I am for money I have my vision pawned
The deep sea of our thought I sold, our expression too I sold

> I traded in religion, in faith too I speculated
> Who said that I only sold love, my lover too I sold

What all I sold, to whom all I sold—in fact, I sold everything
At all times I sold not only myself, but my character too I sold

> I called myself human, but humanity I kept defacing
> *Zair*, the beautiful look of my face, that too I sold

....

Published in *Sheeraza* (Kashmiri) 27:5 (1993), 112.

Bashir "Zair" was born in 1952 in Shurat Kulgam. He studied at the Government School, Kanipora, and at the Government Degree College in Anantnag, and later completed an MA in politics. He taught at Government Higher Secondary School Khoimoh, Kulgam and retired as a lecturer. He writes poetry and short stories.

Ghulam Hassan "Ghamgeen"

Ghazal

Na yeti gul nay chu bulbul nay caman kānh
Na yeti śamhas chu pōnpur gath karan kānh

Tabības gay davāh on khiov barābar
Karith parhēz chunu' dōdu'y balan kānh

Śahar damphuti chi gāmu' ti gām khāmōś
Na jang nāmay na Gulrēzu'y paran kānh

Agar āsī vanun kēnh yiyizi pānay
Yinav qāṣid matav yot sōzu'han kānh

Sahal bālas chu nakh dith jāy badlu'ni
Magar muśkil sŷthā badlun zehan kānh

Sŷthā yatskāli pŷth chum dōd 'aśkun
Yalājī chunu' me ath dādis karan kānh

Ghulam Hassan "Ghamgeen"

Ghazal

No flower here, nor bulbul, nor garden, not even one
Nor does the moth circle the flame here, not even one

We went to the doctor,[1] brought medicine, took it properly
Even after discipline, no disease is cured, not even one

Cities are choked, villages silent
No war epics, no Gulrezs,[2] are read, not even one

If you have something to say, come yourself
Don't you send a messenger here, *matyov*, not even one

Easy to put a shoulder to a hill and shift its location
But very difficult to change a mind, not even one

For a long while, I have been pained by a passion
No healer for this disease, not even one

....

Published in *Aalav* (Srinagar), 11:4 (2007), 50.

Ghulam Hassan "Ghamgeen" was born in 1951 in Srinagar. He has worked as a senior broad-caster in All India Radio (Radio Kashmir). He has published several volumes of writing including *Noorana, Noori Irfan Sanai Nabi* (SAW), *Partavi Anwaar*, and *Mushki Ambar. Seerat Nabi-ur-Rehmah* and *Ashqi Soz* are forthcoming.

NOTES

1. The "doctor" (*tabeeb* in the original) also suggests a person who cures spiritual diseases, including *ishq*.

2. Maqbool Shah Kraalawaari (1820–1877) reworked a Persian Masnavi into the well-known, often sung, Kashmiri love poem *Gulrez*.

A woman holds a photograph of her missing son, days after his body was found on the premises of an Army camp after it was closed down | Delina Baramulla, March 2010

Paramilitary trooper beats a protestor | Nowhatta, Srinagar, January 2009

Kashi Nath "Baghwan"

Ghazal

Tsihis manz kiā samay badliō zamīn tay āsmān badliō
Sọ yāmath āy mehfili manz tu' mehfili hund samān badlẙō

Na badlay sọy na badliō dil na armānan mẙe rang badliō
Me kẙuth bẙhi inqalāb āmut chu patsh kithu' karu' zamān badliō

Mẙe maṣrāvith tu' naṣrāvith agar zan pāsbān badliō
Mạrith rūdus bạ suy yārō faqat mẙōnuy makān badliō

Thazar yāmath dituy vaqtan vanay kiā kiā tse manz badliō
Su dil badlẙō, su sreh badliō yi sōruy chu ayān badliō

Necū yus rāth zāmut chu vanay kiā kiā tạmis badliō
Ạchan manz āb tas badliō, manas lōluk gumān badliō

Sẙṭhā phuṭi naṭi magar az tām zānh mā yāru'bal badliō
Na badli jọy, na badliō bāgh, badliō Bāghwān badliō

Kashi Nath "Baghwan"

Ghazal

In a moment the times changed, the earth and sky changed
When she came into the gathering, the gathering's atmosphere changed

She has not changed, nor have hearts changed, nor the colours of my
desire changed
Then how, in what way, has a revolution come, then how has the world
changed

After forgetting me and driving me mad, if the guardians changed
Even dead I still remain the same, o friends, only my dwelling has
changed

When time granted you standing, what all can I tell you that has in you
changed
That heart changed, that tenderness changed, all that is visible changed

The son who is born to you yesterday, what all can I tell you has for him
changed
The water in his eyes has changed, the feeling of love in the heart has
changed

Many pots have broken but till now never has the watering place[1]
changed
Nor have the brooks changed, nor the gardens changed; if there is
change, it is the *Baghwan* who changed.[2]

....

Published in *Sheeraza* (Kashmiri) 31:4 (1997), 128.

Kashi Nath "Baghwan" (1921–2008) studied at the Mission School, Anantnag, graduated from Sri Pratap College, Srinagar, and took a B.Ed. from Kashmir University. He
taught at the Teachers Training School, Anantnag and retired as principal, Government

Senior Secondary School, Mattan. He wrote on varied themes: devotional songs in *Sharika Daiya*, and sociopolitical issues in *Tuith Nabad*.

NOTES

1. The Kashmiri word *yaarbal* designates that spot on the banks of a river or stream where people gather to wash and chat. It signifies shared conversations and community.

2. *Baghwan*, the poet's *takhallus*, means gardner.

The mother of a disappeared youth during a protest | Srinagar, August 2007

Protestors clash with paramilitary soldiers and police | Srinagar, February 2009

Essay 4

Indian Empire

(and the Case of Kashmir)

This chapter took life as an essay that marked a location and a date: *Srinagar, Jammu and Kashmir, August 15, 2010*. I began by noting the fact that I was analyzing the persistence of colonial modes of thought and forms of governance in postcolonial India while living in a city under constant curfew, where fifty-seven demonstrators had been killed, and many more injured, in police firing in the last three weeks.[1] The date was particularly poignant, as celebrations of Independence Day across the country only emphasized the continuing horror of these weeks in Kashmir. Living in Srinagar, I wrote, brings to a crisis many of the certainties that usually inform postcolonial analyses of an independent nation like India, if only because some of the key terms of anticolonialism articulated by Indian nationalists now inform the intellectual and political framework of activists for the Kashmiri cause. For them, India is the colonial power, the Indian army and paramilitary an occupation force, members of the elected state government are collaborators and stooges of the central government, and bureaucrats, particularly members of all-India civil services, are administrators whose job it is to deny any avenues for Kashmiri self-determination.

Further, Kashmiri nationalists (not unlike their earlier Indian counterparts) make clear that their movement is not simply concerned with economic betterment; in response to both the Prime Minister's and the chief minister's promises of more jobs in the government and in the private sector, they argue that their goal is political self-determination, and that they do not mobilize, and sacrifice their lives, for bread alone. Their movement is for azadi, a word once so dear to Indian anticolonialism, except that it is now the Indian state that thwarts freedom. Kashmiri newspapers sympathetic to the desire for azadi are happy to reprint the work of Indian (and Pakistani) revolutionary poets: where once Sahir Ludhianvi and Faiz Ahmed Faiz spoke out against imperialists, their poems now provide sustenance for the Kashmiri movement as it struggles against Indian domination.

Conversely, the response of the Indian state—the central and state governments and the army and paramilitary forces whose highly intrusive presence warps civilian life in the Kashmir valley—has been to treat the sustained protests in 2015 as a law and order problem, and to crackdown militarily. Even when the prime minister and the home minister have spoken of Kashmir's "unique" status within the Indian union and of the need for an equally unique resolution, their promises lack purpose and conviction, and in any case are treated by Kashmiris as only the latest attempts to mollify widespread political protests and thus to enable a fraudulent, uneasy peace, as has happened repeatedly in recent years. "Mainstream" politicians, that is, elected officials who believe in Jammu and Kashmir's accession to India, lack credibility and are absent from public life; the only political figures who matter today are members of the separatist Hurriyat alliance, with Syed Ali Shah Geelani the most consequential of them. Further, ideologues of Kashmiri independence (or even those who favor achieving the autonomy guaranteed by Article 370 of the Indian Constitution) have developed dense historical accounts of the long Kashmiri struggle against their colonizers that goes back to the sixteenth century (first the Mughal conquest, then Afghan rule, then Sikh, then Dogra, and now Indian). In sum, many of the political and ideological features of classic twentieth-century anticolonial movements are in place in the Kashmiri struggle for self-determination.

This reversal of India's postcolonial credentials is one reason why otherwise progressive Indian intellectuals and politicians have found it so difficult to respond to the challenge posed by Kashmir. We have long assumed the ethical gravitas of being inheritors of a proud anticolonial nationalism, and even though we have developed critiques of the state and of the functioning of democracy in India, we assume that the state, warts and all, is fundamentally *postcolonial* in its self-conception and functioning. That is, we are convinced that the actions of politicians, bureaucrats, and police and military officials vis-à-vis particular communities, no matter how polarized, are analytically comprehensible within an analysis of the problems of a young democracy. Thus, we document the travails of significant sectors of our democracy very well: our newspapers and magazines are full of exposés of corruption and official malfeasance, but also of substantive debates about the misappropriation of natural resources, tax revenues, or the developmental capacities of the state.

However, in other areas of governance, the self-righteous and aggressive nationalism bred by our anticolonial history has caused us to blunt our critiques of state functioning. Precisely because we demonstrated against and dethroned an empire, we like to believe that independence inaugurated a fundamentally different form of sovereign, constitutional rule that safeguards the state from assuming any of the attributes of the colonial state. No longer do imperial viceroys rule subjects; now elected officials rule in the name, and with the electoral consent, of citizens. In key areas, however, the Indian state has confirmed and enhanced the doctrines and methods it had inherited from British colonial law and policy. Prime among these is the dogma that once the departing British had defined the external boundaries of the nation (however opportunistically and inexactly, and many were not defined at all), the populations contained within them were not to be allowed the right to political self-determination. These boundaries were to be defended at all costs, not only against external enemies, but also against secessionist movements or movements seeking different forms of autonomy.

That is, rather than the state functioning as the prime agency that would encourage citizens to evolve more progressive and equitable power-sharing arrangements across the nation, the state acts primarily to preserve the boundaries of the union in the form inherited from the British empire. This is true even when there are reasons to believe that this cartographic inheritance had been crafted without considering the needs and particular histories of local populations, and even if the policing required for the maintenance of borders involves the suspension of fundamental principles of democratic functioning. Thus one of the cardinal features of state-formation in the independent nation has become the development of a massive security apparatus ostensibly designed to guard international borders, but in effect to act internally against restive populations contained, by the force of historical circumstance, within those borders. Indeed, one might argue that this security apparatus, developed under the cover of an aggressive, celebratory nationalism, is an important element of the postcolonial state's claims to legitimacy.

This chapter will ask what the history of modern empire and of state-formation within it can teach us about the formation and functioning of the state in formally decolonized, independent nations like India. It will also consider the converse of this question: Can an analysis of the centrality of a particular kind of state-formation to the making of empire help us understand some of the deeply undemocratic imperatives and neocolonial ambitions of the postcolonial nation-state today? I will argue that crucial modes of governance, particularly the relation between the militarized state and its subject populations that characterized colonial empires, extend into the present moment. European imperial nations established colonies via battle and conquest, as the British (East India Company) did after 1757 in India, and held and expanded their territorial holdings by building large armies using revenues and taxes raised from the subjects they ruled. This territorial and military legacy was inherited, in a "transfer of power," by the government of a newly independent India, which renewed both colonial legislation and colonial attitudes in order to deal with challenges to its authority, particularly from populations at its peripheries who wished to choose their own form of national (or even subnational) political formation. Further, as India achieves global economic heft, the policing functions of the state, far from being whittled down, are in fact being rapidly enhanced to deal not only with problems at the borders, but also with any form of resistance mounted by mobilized citizens within, whether these be communities protesting large scale industrialization that displaces and alienates them from their livelihood, or people who wish to call sharp attention to the age-old socioeconomic structures that are responsible for their historical dispossession.

....

INDIA'S "NEOCOLONIAL AMBITIONS"

I will begin not with matters at home, so to speak, but with an explanation of the appropriateness of a phrase I used earlier, India's "neocolonial ambitions." I take my cue from a recent article by C. Raja Mohan, the then "strategic affairs editor" of the *Indian Express*, and a former holder of the Henry A. Kissinger Chair in Foreign Policy and International Relations at the John W. Kluge Center, Library of Congress. Mohan outlines a remarkable vision of military cooperation between the United States of America and India. He argues that "the Obama Administration needs to elevate the bilateral military engagement with India to a strategic level," because "a rising India," will be "a more credible and sustainable partner" than Western Europe or Japan in "coping with new international security challenges." If both the United States and India "can shake off the remaining historical baggage that has kept them at arm's length for most of the past sixty years, we may see something remotely like the return of the Raj" (2010). The "return of the Raj"? But before we examine the many assumptions about history and colonialism that make the revival of that political condition imaginable, let alone desirable, we might briefly summarize the contextual historical developments that encourage an Indian security strategist to reach for that quite astonishing phrase. Mohan's ideas about such "bilateralism" are no longer singular: the unprecedented growth of the Indian economy in the last decade, as well as the rise to global prominence of Indian multinational enterprises, has encouraged political theorists and policy planners to imagine a world in which India emerges as a regional power, with the military capacity (particularly a blue water or expeditionary navy) to enforce its foreign policy agendas and economic interests, as well as to play a more visible role in international peace keeping. This model of regional authority has been developed in tandem with, and in imagined opposition to, the even more prominent rise of China as an economic power.[2]

There is of course another crucial longer-term geopolitical development that explains Mohan's invitation to India to function as a regional satrap of US global power. After the formal dissolution of the Soviet Union in 1991, regional alliances built by the United States and the Soviets, including those represented by the "non-aligned" nations, began to redefine themselves. Nations that shifted their affiliations included some of the constituent republics of the Soviet Union, nations in Europe that had belonged to COMECON and the Warsaw Pact, and nations in Africa and Asia that had communist governments or were recipients of aid from the Soviet Union, and that often followed its lead at the United Nations. This decade also saw important milestones in the formal decolonization of the globe, particularly the 1994 general elections in South Africa that demolished the last bastion of racist white European empire in Africa. In this new world, empires of the most visible sort (those based on direct territorial control, the subordination of majority populations, and the extraction of surplus to enrich colonizers or the colonizing nation) seemed a thing of the past. For a brief moment, it also seemed as if empire as an ideal of governance, or as a desirable model of economic organization, no longer had currency or legitimacy.

However, the intermeshed world that modern European imperialists had created between the seventeenth and twentieth centuries, based upon hierarchical economic, political, and cultural relations between colonizers and those colonized, did not alter quickly or considerably. Once-colonized nations now controlled their political futures (though their colonial masters were prone to influence developments, or even to intervene), but they certainly were not welcome to entirely rewrite trading arrangements bequeathed to them by their erstwhile rulers. Indeed in most cases the nationalist elites who had led the struggle for political independence saw no reason at all to abrogate ways of doing business that would continue to enrich them. This was the case even in India, for all the fact that its economy, for three decades after independence, was centrally planned and most of its key sectors closed off to foreign capital. Given protected and captive markets, indigenous capital grew in volume and this growth, coupled with the successful development of technically skilled engineers and managers, allowed Indians the confidence to find their place within an international technomanagerial and commercial ruling class. In the last two decades, Indians participating in the global networks of capital have also consolidated their power at home. The process of economic liberalization initiated in 1991—and the creation of a massive and deeply uneven consumer economy—required the formal repudiation of the institutional mechanisms of nationalist or socialist modes of economic organization.

In effect, in this process of globalization, the economic agendas and protocols dictated by once-colonizing capitalist nations became the state doctrines of once-colonized nations. Multilateral agencies like the World Bank, the International Monetary Fund, the General Agreement on Tariffs and Trade, and the World Trade Organization played a crucial role; they legislated and enforced particular mechanisms of economic and commercial development, while denying the legitimacy of public sector or state-managed enterprises, and of state-subsidized programs of poverty alleviation or the redistribution of wealth. Globalization has of course taken some surprising turns: few could have predicted the rise of multinational capitalists and corporations from countries like Russia, China, and India, nor the sporadically spectacular growth rate of the Indian and Chinese economies, particularly at a time when the most powerful economies in the West have struggled. Economists now believe that well before 2050 China will be the largest national economy, and that Russia, Brazil, and India will play roles in the global economy larger than that of the European Union. Particularly after several years of recession in the West, the world is changing rapidly, with new centers of economic power in view and realignments of economic relations across the globe.

However, all these developments are taking place in the context of a unipolar world, with a single superpower, the United States, continuing to intervene diplomatically and militarily in situations deemed a challenge to its authority.[3] We now have what seems to be a confusing scenario: the United States maintains its ability to fight two overseas wars at one time, as well as its ring of military bases across the globe, while at the same time struggling to revive its domestic economy. As several commentators have noted, these developments suggest that at this moment in its history the United States is slipping inevitably into the decline that defined its precursor empire, Great Britain, where the contradiction between its blighted post–World War II economy and its military capacity contributed to the success of the anticolonial movements that brought about the end of empire.

But the model of "informal" empire represented by the US is different. American power across the globe has been based not so much upon territorial acquisition overseas as upon economic and diplomatic power backed by the ability, and the will, to intervene militarily. For more than a century now, from the Spanish-American War of 1898 to Iraq and Afghanistan today, the United States has fought wars across the globe and has carved out spheres of influence that it polices from its bases and embassies overseas. By one estimate, in 2001 the United States had bases in more than sixty countries and overseas territories.[4] As the editors of the *Monthly Review* put it, "U.S. global political, economic, and financial power . . . require the periodic exercise of military power. The other advanced capitalist countries tied into this system have also become reliant on the United States as the main enforcer of the rules of the game. The positioning of U.S. military bases should therefore be judged not as a purely military phenomenon, but as a mapping out of the U.S.-dominated imperial sphere and of its spearheads within the periphery" (2002). Even as twentieth-century decolonization movements across the globe spelled the end of modern European empires, and to that extent the decline of empire as an ideology of international political and economic organization, the US's informal empire continues to thrive, and has become the (much-debated, to be sure) exemplar of international power and authority.

Thus, to return to Mohan's article, it is scarcely surprising that the "imagination of empire", as it were, still holds security analysts in its thrall. And not only security analysts, for as is well known by now, a number of historians and economists have gained public notice by advocating an aggressive role for the United States and its surrogates across the globe: military intervention, policing, the management of economies and populations, are all seen to be part of the renewed mandate for empire. Niall Ferguson was the poster boy for such neoconservatism, particularly in his insistence that the United States, as a leader of a coalition or on its own, ought to occupy and manage countries that are not quite amenable—for any number of reasons—to Washington's view of the world (see for example Ferguson 2003).[5] This and similar attempts to get the United States to formalize its informal empire, were remarkably short-lived: neoconservative imperialists have not had direct influence upon the Obama administration, though Obama has continued with the expansion of the US military presence overseas.[6] United States foreign policy remains committed to the unilateral determination, and the protection, of United States interests, particularly its access to commodities and markets, and there is no sign of a scaling back of US bases across the globe.[7]

In this scenario, Mohan's priorities are clear: India should have a special bilateral relation with the United States, which will entail, in part, functioning under its aegis as a regional power. But why would Mohan reach toward raj revivalism (he calls it a "creative renewal" of the "Raj legacy") in order to most vividly illustrate his sense that India, and its army and navy, should be put at the service of the United States, and to be sure, of parallel Indian interests? Is this simply an idiosyncratic and attention-grabbing formulation or is there more at stake here? For Mohan, the British raj in India demonstrated what he identifies as the " 'India Center' that organized peace and stability in much of the Eastern Hemisphere during the nineteenth and twentieth centuries."[8] In order for him to claim British imperial history as a precedent for an Indian future, Mohan resorts to a rhetorical sleight of hand: for him, it is always a national entity called

India, and not an imperial state, British India, that acts to police colonial territories. Where others might see a fundamental political and foreign policy break between British India and an independent Republic of India, Mohan offers seamless continuity. In fact, he claims to redress the unfortunate legacy of an anti-imperialist postcolonial politics here: "it is not just the West that is ignorant of the security legacy of the British Raj; India's own post-colonial political class deliberately induced a collective national amnesia about the country's rich pre-independence military traditions. Its foreign policy establishment still pretends that India's engagement with the world began on August 15, 1947."

Administrators of the British Empire used troops from India, paid for by Indian taxpayers without of course any mechanism to ascertain their approval (we are talking about empire here) to police, as well as to gain and hold, colonial territories in sites ranging from Egypt and Iraq to Malaya and South Africa, as well as to fight in Europe and elsewhere in both World War I and II.[9] Rather than pose a problem for Mohan, this fundamentally undemocratic exercise in imperial warmongering provides an argument for the future. He confidently asserts that, were Obama to upgrade the US's strategic alliance with India, he will find in "Manmohan Singh [then Prime Minister of India] a partner who is ready to work with the United States in constituting a postcolonial Raj that can bear the burdens of ordering the Eastern Hemisphere in the 21st century." In his argument, a "postcolonial Raj" not only entails the extension of Indian power overseas, but also the willing addition of Indian military resources to the US arsenal (even a "postcolonial Raj" needs its Raja, after all). The postcolonial future thus reiterates the colonial past, except that a sovereign India now acts in strategic accordance with the foreign policy and commercial imperatives of the global military power, the United States.[10]

....

THE LEGACIES OF EMPIRE

The historical legacy of empire, as well as its perpetuation in the present moment in an imperial formation like that maintained by the US across the globe, continues to structure international relations in spite of the rise of other national or collective centers of economic power (such as the European Union). In any case, the mode of "development" that has allowed the economic growth of China or Brazil or India in the last two decades is largely an extension of the capitalist forms of resource exploitation put into place by imperial European nations between the eighteenth and the late-twentieth centuries (China of course was never colonized, but crucial sectors of its economy were "internationalized" by the sea-borne power of Britain, as for instance in the First and Second Opium Wars). Today, transnational corporations originating in any of these nations, or indeed anywhere in the world, operate in similar ways, and are backed by national governments in their search for resources, labor, and markets. As human populations and needs grow and consumer economies deplete resources worldwide, the future seems increasingly competitive and fraught, particularly given that there is no international effort to bring into being cooperative or more equitable forms of development. The earth's ecology cannot support the extension of the standard of living of the ex-colonial powers to people everywhere, and it is clear that technological solutions today cannot enable anything like a reasonable standard of living across the globe. Certainly there are now "middle class" populations in most nations that share in a global consumer culture, but this level of consumption simply cannot be made available to the world's population. In this scenario, the future suggests greater class polarization within nations, and greater antagonism between nations as they compete internationally for resources and markets.

The compact between trading corporations and states was a product, and indeed an enabler, of modern European empires. After the territorial gains made by Spanish conquistadors in the Americas, and the establishing of commercial silver mining there, European colonialism and capitalism were both enabled by chartered companies (the Dutch Vereenigde Oost-Indische Compagnie, the English East India Company, the Royal African Company). These early national companies with transnational interests and power were legally authorized to act militarily in the name of the state. They were also the precursors of modern transnational corporations; indeed many of the most powerful contemporary transnational corporations began their international operations, and grew to their enormous scope, as extensions of European and United States colonial power. Colonial control offered resources, labor, and markets that these companies exploited; profits were repatriated to Europe.[11] Decolonization complicated matters for these corporations, but their global power overrode their dubious, occasionally criminal, legacy, and in some key cases, when democratic regimes made attempts to nationalize their operations, they were destabilized by a combination of corporate and ex-colonial state power.[12] In any case, over time transnational corporations and decolonized nations have established relations that are simultaneously symbiotic (the former need the legal cover and access to land made available by the latter, the latter need technology and skills, as well as tax revenues) and contentious (as in the past, questions of sovereignty are often at stake). The terms of this coexistence are becoming more complex as even small corporations internationalize their supply chains and their markets; and now nations like India too are readying to back "their" transnational corporations both in terms of strategic foreign policies and, if it comes to that, militarily. The nation, far from receding as an actor in an world of transnational capital flows and increasing globalization, now plays an even more active role to generate both domestic and foreign policy to suit corporate trading and industrial interests.

The nation-state as a political formation, and as an actor on the world stage, is a comparatively recent phenomenon, and it is worth remembering that the bulk of nation-states across the globe are products of empire. (This is true even of many imperial nations: for instance, Great Britain came into being in the seventeenth and eighteenth century via the forced and unequal assimilation of Ireland and Scotland, a process Daniel Hechter (1999) has described as "internal colonialism.") In the Americas, Africa, and Asia there were certainly interlinked forms of political and economic collectivity before European colonization, but the boundaries of nations as they exist today are more often than not the creation of imperial governance, or of corresponding processes of decolonization. Given this provenance of the nation-state, it is extraordinary how much power it exerts, both materially and ideologically, to define, limit, and mobilize populations. However, it is perhaps even more extraordinary how much effort nation-states expend to police elements of their population who do not identify—or are not allowed to identify—with the nation, and who, for a variety of reasons, are not empowered as full citizens. Ironically, this is the case even within postcolonial democratic nations, where the electoral system that grants each adult a vote does not compensate for other historical forms of marginalization suffered by large sections, occasionally even majorities, of their citizens.

To that extent, independent India's security establishment has been built not only to counter Pakistan (with which it has fought three wars) and China (one war), or—and this is a recent possibility—to extend its power across oceans, but also to coerce its own populations into maintaining the borders drawn precipitously, inexactly, and often unfairly by the departing British colonial administration. For instance, in October 1947, when the Indian Army and Air Force flew into Srinagar to repel tribal irregulars originating from western Kashmir and Pakistan (and thus incorporated sections of the princely state of Jammu and Kashmir into India), the Indian state extended its frontiers, but also put into place systems that denied large sections of the Kashmiri population the right to determine their own political identity, a problem that continues to fester.[13] In other "border" campaigns in the Northeast, the Indian state continues to deploy the army and paramilitaries against tribal populations who wish for sovereign and independent homelands in Nagaland, Mizoram, and Manipur. In the last three decades, state boundaries have been redrawn in that region to accommodate local demands, but any attempts to carve out independent or even autonomous homelands have been put down, often brutally, by the army and paramilitary forces (for an overview, see Hazarika 1994). In each case political processes and civil governance have been routinely marginalized to allow military "solutions."[14] Most recently, rather than imagine viable political options, the Union Home Ministry has initiated combat operations against the Naxalite movement operating in central India. Within the government, the primary debate seems to be whether these operations should be conducted by central paramilitary and state police forces or if the army and the air force should also be inducted into this combat.

As this account suggests, India is no stranger to the use of the army and the paramilitary against its own populations. If Great Britain and the United States, the two dominant imperial powers of the last two centuries, offer any precedents, they are that empire-building is a process that requires the suppression (the forced amalgamation) of populations *within* as much as elsewhere.[15] The bloody history of the expansion of the United States across the North American continent, which entailed the destruction of Native American and Spanish-Mexican communities, as well as the systematic abuse of African slave labor, are too well known to require retelling here. England established its colonies in Ireland in the late sixteenth century (see Canny 1988, 2001), and held them for the next two-hundred-and-fifty years (parts of Northern Ireland are still part of the United Kingdom). The 1706 Act of Union united Scotland and England into an Anglocentric kingdom, but the highlands of Scotland still needed brutal "pacification" via the anti-Jacobite campaigns of 1715 and 1745.[16] One of the consequences of the systematic dispossession of the Irish and of the destruction of the Scottish clan system was that disproportionate numbers of Irish and Scottish peasants emigrated to Britain's trans-Atlantic colonies and provided the manpower for Britain's armies abroad. In many ways then, Britain's colonialism, like that of the United States, began at home.

The political mentality and methods of the modern imperial state are a product of these twin processes: the state hones its capacity for military violence at home even as it projects it across its borders. Further, these nation-states offer their marginalized subjects (particularly those who have resisted their territorial and political authority) a simple bargain: accept the suzerainty of the state and the centralized control of economic development (including those made available by access to opportunities in captive markets abroad) or be constantly at the receiving end of state surveillance and military action. (This is one of the purposes of raising larger and more numerous paramilitary forces, where the local and regional identities of recruits are subordinated into a highly disciplined form of nation-centricism. Equally important, recruits from one state or region are used to police populations in others; cultural, linguistic, and occasionally, religious differences between paramilitaries and locals enable more militaristic and uncaring forms of intervention.) The logic and history of the colonial state inform the structures of postcolonial governance to a point where they stunt any possibility of political thought and action that respects modes of collective being other than those defined by a coercive form of national belonging. But this cannot be understood simply as a problem of inheritance: postcolonial governance takes the forms that it does because the state's developed capacity for violence is crucial to organize the exploitation of economic resources at home as well as abroad. Colonial forms of territorial control and trade reshaped the globe to make resources and products available in ways that disproportionately enriched imperialists and enhanced socioeconomic distortions among colonized peoples; postcolonial governance refines these methods, only now in the name of national development.[17]

The point here is that the advocacy of India's potential global power, or at least regional military authority (the "India center" theorized by the colonial administrator Olaf Caroe), is in fact an advocacy of the power, and the right, of the putatively postcolonial state to insist upon quintessentially colonial territorial, political, and economic arrangements. The mentality and methods of empire live on, and political processes that might subject them to local self-determination are delegitimized ideologically and denied militarily. There is a great irony here, for most twentieth-century anti-imperialist movements recognized that *decolonization* demanded not only political independence for colonized nations but also a fundamental rethinking of more local sociocultural and political practices that had been historically malformed by imperialism. In practice however, an independent nation-state like India acts upon lessons in governance taught by the empire of which it was once a part: the writ of the centralizing state is forcefully extended over all populations within its (often poorly defined) borders, even if those populations had never participated in creating, or have never acknowledged the legitimacy of, those borders. An India with global power aspirations, indeed an India that plans to translate its economic power and large population into the capacity to police its neighbors across the Indian Ocean and the Arabian Sea, is a nation that is not predisposed to allow equitable arrangements within its borders. This is true even of peaceful mass movements to resist centralized, hierarchical decision making, whether these involve people displaced by big dams that bring no value to their communities, or indeed by mining or other industrial corporations that dispossess peasants and tribals of their traditional livelihoods without offering corresponding benefits.[18] Peaceful protest movements, as well as the constitutional process that recognizes their moral legitimacy and indeed political authority, are collateral damage to the onslaught of the twinned powers of the state and multinational capital.

....

THE UNFINISHED BUSINESS OF KASHMIR

The terms and claims of this analysis so far have been sweeping; and this chapter more a polemical overview of historical developments and state formation rather than a particular instance of the methods of governance of the colonial/independent state. In what remains of this chapter I will call attention to Kashmir, and in particular to the muscular forging of its recent history by India (and to a lesser extent by Pakistan). Kashmiris have at best been reluctant participants in crucial episodes of supposedly democratic politics and governance post-1947, and in important ways their opinions have been disregarded in the same way as they were during the autocratic rule of the Dogra maharajas, who ruled as vassals of the British raj. Twentieth-century Kashmiri history features largely poor peasants, pastoralists, and forest dwellers ruled by feudal landlords (Muslims, Hindus, and Sikhs) with little interest in alleviating the poverty or illiteracy of their subjects. Dogra rule favoured Hindu and Sikh administrators and confirmed the gap between them and the mass of Muslim (and Hindu) peasants (Rai 2004). Only after Sheikh Abdullah's National Conference came to power was rural landholding restructured in favor of the tiller. School and college education were made free, and in its "Naya Kashmir" manifesto, the state government articulated (if not always enacted) its progressive social vision.

In 1947, the maharaja's forced and precipitous accession (which, apart from anything else, denied the principle of the merger of majority populations in contiguous territories that supposedly governed the demarcation of borders in the Partition process) led to the de facto partitioning of the erstwhile princely state into Indian (Jammu, Kashmir, and Ladakh) and Pakistani (Kashmir, Gilgit, and Baltistan) sectors. It also created a political situation where relations between India and this new Indian state were mired in suspicion. For Indian (and Pakistani) administrators, Kashmir remained unfinished business; for India this meant that any Kashmiri politician who spoke in the name of self-determination, or indeed acted to confirm the autonomy granted by Article 370 of the constitution was deeply suspect. Thus the Indian state would countenance no political arrangements other than those premised upon the heavily militarized line of control functioning effectively as a border between India and Pakistan. That this border, as other lines on the map drawn in 1947 to demarcate India from East Pakistan, and indeed India from Burma and China, disrupted traditional communities and trade routes in Ladakh, Kashmir, and in Jammu was of no consideration: the postcolonial state was determined to enforce the boundaries it inherited from its colonial predecessor.

For a precarious new Indian government, battered by the enormous challenges of Partition violence and the need to resettle massive numbers of displaced people, among other more routine problems of governance, one of the bases of its legitimacy became its ability to police its borders as well as any populations who saw those borders not as sacrosanct, but as contingent, as the products of political chicanery and compromise. Over time—and Pakistan played its own partisan role here—the borders of

Jammu and Kashmir provided a powerful rationale for the development of a massive (and for a nation that contains the largest number of the world's poor, unconscionable) security apparatus. Since independence, the army, air force, Border Security Force, and Central Reserve Police Force have seen a vast (and largely unquestioned) expansion, and more specialized units like the Assam Rifles and the Rashtriya Rifles (raised in 1990) are dedicated to fighting secessionist insurgencies in Assam and its adjoining areas and in J & K respectively. The ill-equipped army's ignominious retreat in the face of Chinese troops in 1962, and wars against Pakistan in 1965 and 1971, meant that military and paramilitary budgets became disproportionately large well before India began to aspire to regional power status; this was the case even in the years when India claimed Gandhian pacifism and non-alignment as crucial pillars of its foreign policy.

······················

ELECTORAL DEMOCRACY?

Between 1948 and 1989, Kashmiris rode a political roller coaster: elected governments, led largely by Sheikh Abdullah's National Conference, came to power, but neither they nor the Indian government made any attempts to find an equitable solution for the structural problem of a polity brought into being by a disputed accession and enforced borders. India's fig leaf lay in its stated position, argued before the United Nations, that it would conduct a plebiscite, but only once Pakistan had withdrawn from what India called "Pakistan Occupied Kashmir," so that all the populations of the Dogra maharaja's kingdom could participate. (The irony here is immediately obvious: a postcolonial state arguing that the only democratic political action it could contemplate was one based on respecting the territorial contours of a feudal regime crafted in wars and authorized by the British empire.) In 1953, on the first occasion that Sheikh Abdullah, the elected prime minister, sought to explore the possibility of a Kashmir less tied to India's political and economic control, he was arrested (he was to spend almost twenty years in jail). At each point the Indian bogey was that any moves toward autonomy were in fact covert moves toward an alliance or amalgamation with Pakistan, and that inchoate threat was enough for the Indian central government to intervene undemocratically. There were of course several political parties that were pro-Pakistan, and stood for union with it, but none of them were allowed any significant presence in the state assembly or the Indian parliament. On the obverse, there was no shortage of Kashmiri politicians and people of influence who decided—opportunistically or out of conviction—that their future lay with India.

An electoral system did emerge, fitfully in many areas (there were elections to the state assembly in which administrative officials decided on the single candidate, who was then duly elected), more robustly in others, but elections were always supervised to make certain that no anti-India politicians were elected.[19] In 1977, for the first time, free elections were held, and a Sheikh Abdullah-led National Conference won a majority (forty-seven out of seventy-two seats, with the Janata Party and the Congress winning thirteen and eleven, respectively, largely from the Jammu region. The 1983 elections were considered to be largely fair too, and a Farooq Abdullah-led National Conference retained power, but the return of Indira Gandhi as prime minister meant the renewal of unabashed central intervention in J&K, and she dismissed this government a year later, installing one that she preferred. But worse lay ahead: even though Farooq Abdullah and then Prime Minister Rajiv Gandhi had signed an electoral pact between the National Conference and the Congress, they were so fearful of the Muslim United Front (MUF), a new political alliance that included pro-Pakistan parties, that the elections of 1987 were massively rigged).

Sumit Ganguly (1996) provides a succinct comment on these elections and their consequences:

In this election, voters were intimidated, ballot boxes tampered with, and candidates threatened. Whereas previous generations of Kashmiris, whose political consciousness was low, had long tolerated all manner of electoral irregularities, the generation that had emerged in Kashmir during the long years of Sheikh Abdullah's incarceration did not have the same regard for the Abdullah family, nor was it willing to tolerate such widespread electoral fraud. Indeed, it is rather telling that several key insurgent leaders, Shabir Shah, Yasin Malik, and Javed Mir, were polling agents for the Muslim United Front in the 1987 elections. . . . The extensive electoral malfeasances that they witnessed in 1987 convinced this younger generation of Kashmiris that the national government in New Delhi had scant regard for their political rights and reckless disregard for democratic procedures. With no other institutional recourse open for expressing their disenchantment with the flawed political process, they resorted to violence.

It is also worth noting that Syed Salahuddin (then known as Mohammed Yusuf Shah), the present Pakistan-based head of the Hizb-ul-Mujahiddin, was a MUF candidate in these elections. He was arrested from the vote counting hall and jailed for the next nine months for protesting the rigging; upon his release, he too crossed into Pakistan, and into the leadership of a militant group financed and trained by Pakistanis.

This brief account of election history in Jammu and Kashmir is of course not meant to be an adequate explanation for the events of 1989 and after, when pitched battles began between militants (both Kashmiris and non-Kashmiri recruits from the Afghan war against the Soviets) and the Indian army, paramilitary, and police forces. My attempt here is simply to underline the fact that elections, which are the guarantors of democracy and thus of the legitimacy of state power, were routinely suborned by the Indian central government (and their Kashmiri collaborators, to be sure) in pursuit of a malleable state administration. All this was done in the name of national security, of safeguarding the mainland's territorial interests by foreclosing the possibility of Kashmir becoming either an effectively autonomous, independent, or Pakistani state. In effect the state's location has caused its people to be held hostage to the Indian government's sense that, post-Partition, no more territory was to be ceded to Pakistan or indeed to be allowed to define itself differently from the nationalist conception underlying the Indian Union. There is also the question of demography: as the only Muslim-majority state in India (with a sizeable Hindu, Buddhist, and Sikh population), an Indian Jammu and Kashmir is supposedly a shining instance of the secular values enshrined in the constitution.

Since India's independence, prolonged mass agitation, or changing demographics, have led to the demarcation of new states (Gujarat, Nagaland, Haryana, Himachal Pradesh, Uttarakhand, Chattisgarh, Jharkhand, now Telengana), but no argument for independence or functional autonomy was (or is) allowed to stand. Indeed, the forms of autonomy prescribed for J&K by Article 370 have slowly been whittled down, resulting in the even greater alienation of Kashmiris, and the revival of mass mobilizations demanding not just functional autonomy but azadi. Further, for more than two decades now, Kashmir has suffered the consequences of an oppressive military and paramilitary footprint.[20] To take two instances of the way in which democratic processes and ordinary codes of policing are suspended here, we might consider that the J&K Police are quick to invoke the Public Safety Act, which allows them to incarcerate citizens for up to a year, and in jails outside the state. Similarly, the Indian Army has operated since 1990 under the Armed Forces Special Powers Act (AFSPA), which has allowed the military great latitude and virtual impunity in its dealings with the local population.[21]

Even after the army announced that the armed militancy of the 1990s has dwindled into sporadic skirmishes, recent attempts to withdraw or amend this deeply repressive, even unconstitutional act are met with immediate opposition. In a deliberately provocative statement, one senior general insisted that the AFSPA was the army's "holy book" and must not be lifted, even if some army officers and soldiers misused its provisions (NDTV; see also "Demand for Changes . . ."). In practice, this act places army actions outside of civilian legal review; not surprisingly, it has its origins in British colonial law, which regulated subjects, not citizens. In August 1942, in the face of the massive Quit India movement, Lord Linlithgow, then viceroy, enacted the Armed Forces Special Powers Ordinance to allow the police and army exceptional powers against civilians. This is the ordinance that became the basis for independent India's enactment of the Armed Forces (Special Powers) Act, 1958, to provide legal cover for inhumane army operations in Assam and Manipur.[22] In sum, a colonial ordinance designed to legalize what were considered, even by colonial standards, extraordinary military methods designated to quell a nationalist anticolonial movement was revived and strengthened by independent India to legalize extraordinary military methods to repress political movements among sections of the population at its peripheries.[23]

. . . .

KASHMIR IN THE NATIONALIST-IDEOLOGICAL IMAGINATION

The "problem" of Kashmir for independent India should not however be understood simply as a failure of democratic governance or of the punitive deployment of colonial policing and military methods. I have mentioned some of the ideological, that is, nationalist reasons, why different constituencies and political parties in India insist that Kashmir is an inalienable part of the nation. For the Bharatiya Janata Party, the primary proponents of hardline nationalism, no territory must be ceded to secessionists, center-state relations (no matter how iniquitous) must not be rethought, and no limits should be imposed on the power of the army or paramilitaries for fear of damaging their morale (any amendment of the AFSPA, for example, will be seen as a tacit admission of its misuse by the army). The Congress is less publicly committed to such an unyielding response but it too treats Kashmir as a problem in governance rather than as the occasion for any sustained rethinking about the political forms of autonomy in the state or indeed federalism in India. Communist parliamentarians have called for a reassessment of India's security regime in Kashmir, but they too have not encouraged any full-blown debate about center-state relations, especially if the centerpiece of this debate is to be a border state like Kashmir.

In each case, one of the unstated assumptions that guides Indian political thinking about Jammu, Ladakh, and Kashmir is that this region represents a palimpsestic history, where the confluence of Buddhism, Hinduism, and Islam has created a cultural texture that is particularly "Indian." This certainly is a laudable religio-cultural ideal, but not when it is asserted to repress the socioeconomic history of the state since at least the mid-nineteenth century, which features the struggle of the impoverished majority for their economic, human, and political rights. And if anything, the last two decades have meant that many, if not the largest mass of Kashmiris, have looked anywhere but to their south for cultural, religious, and political orientation. If idealized notions of a syncretic past supposedly anchor the Indian political imagination, visions of the future make clear to Indian planners that Kashmir is crucial for their access to the Central Asian nations as well as to their geostrategic links with Afghanistan and Iran (and indeed to their "containment" of Pakistan to the north and west and China to the east and north). It is in fact the case that the borders (or rather, the lines of control) between India, Pakistan, and China in that region are unsettled and provide repeated occasions for posturing, sabre rattling, and skirmishing. These borders are among the most heavily militarized in the world, which means that civilians in the state bear the full weight of this military presence, even when it is ostensibly directed across international borders.

We should also remember that there are also very powerful material reasons for India to possess Kashmir (or indeed for Pakistan to hold its sections of the erstwhile state of Jammu and Kashmir). I will not elaborate on these here, as many of these details are under-researched or hidden in official secrecy, but will call attention to some salient issues. There are hydrocarbon deposits—oil and gas—though there has not been much exploration or drilling in the last two decades because of violence in the state (see Narayan and Jayaswal 2010; Suri 2009). Ladakh is likely to contain rare minerals of a variety of sorts, though it is not yet clear whether these are extensive enough to reward mining ("Uranium Deposits..."). However, as India expands its investments in nuclear power and weaponry, the importance of exploitable uranium and thorium deposits cannot be underestimated. Perhaps most important at this moment is the question of water resources. Ever since Partition, India and Pakistan have quarreled over the usage of the waters of the five rivers that flow into Punjab. The 1960 Indus Water Treaty, signed under the aegis of the World Bank, achieved a tenuous accord—which seems to have worked so far—as regards water sharing (for a overview from the Indian point of view, see Sridhar 2005). In recent years, Indian hydroelectric projects (and the development of catchment areas and water-control mechanisms) have polarized matters again, and Pakistani leaders, aware that the origins of rivers in the Indian region of Kashmir gives India great strategic leverage, have protested vociferously (see Mirani 2009). As Mirani points out, India is clear about the "geostrategic and foreign policy implications" of its hydroelectrical projects in Kashmir. Mirani also points to a further wrinkle: India has refused to allow the Jammu and Kashmir state government to build and operate dams like the Kishenganga and Baglihar projects, which have been commissioned and built by the National Hydro Power Corporation, thus ensuring central control over the production and distribution of electricity, to the detriment of both the state exchequer and its consumers of electricity.[24]

In all these ways, Kashmir represents a fundamental political challenge to the democratic functioning of the postcolonial nation-state (but certainly not a unique challenge, as the histories of Naga and Manipuri self-assertion illustrate). So far, the state's response to this challenge has been twofold: to make central funds available in an effort to demonstrate to Kashmiris the benefits of affiliation with India, and to maintain a massive repressive apparatus whose violent actions warn of the futility of independent thought and action.[25] The former has not worked, certainly not entirely or convincingly, and the latter has been disastrous. I will not here suggest possible solutions: an entire army of politicians, administrators, and experts continue to work on what seems to be an intractable polarization between state and people, Indian nationalism and Kashmiri self-determination. But I will remind us, as concerned citizens, that we have a proud history of progressive ideas, those that fed the politics of decolonization, to draw upon, ideas that insisted that the evolution of our independent, egalitarian democracy was an ongoing process, open-ended in its possibilities, and constantly aware of the need to develop and respect modes of self-determination, including those at odds with conventional political wisdom. Such openness—an openness to a genuinely *postcolonial* future—will be of great consequence not only to India but also to the world community in which it plays an increasingly consequential role. If we are to continue to desire and bring into being democratic and egalitarian forms of human development across the globe, we should realize that that effort too begins at home.

NOTES

1. This number kept mounting; newspapers finally reported 110 people killed in this period of unrest. They stopped counting the numbers shot and maimed.

2. China's ambitions are clear from its state-sponsored investments in commodity-rich nations in Africa, its development of the deep-water port of Gwadar in southwest Pakistan, and its enhanced trading relations with Latin American nations. China has also invested enormous resources into its nuclear submarines, new aircraft carriers, and bases that are able to shelter and service them, with the result that believers in realpolitik insist that it is only a matter of time before China challenges the domination of the United States in sea lanes and territories ranging from Africa to Australia. See for instance Thomas Harding's report on the Sanya base on Hainan Island (2008).

India's help in developing the Iranian port of Chabahar, which allows easy access to the Indian Ocean, is seen as an attempt to outflank the Chinese and Pakistani development of Gwadar, and to allow the unhindered movement of goods and natural resources from Iran, Afghanistan, and the Central Asian republics.

3. Ironically, one of the symptoms of the weakened US economy is the high percentage of its public debt held by central banks in China and Japan (and several other countries) that have made massive investments in US treasury securities. Such investments reflect confidence in the ability of the United States to repay its debts over time, but they are also made for other pragmatic reasons (China for instance needs US consumers for the burgeoning export-driven sectors of its economy).

4. Estimate by the editors of the *Monthly Review*; for analysis and a map showing these locations, see "US Military Bases and Empire," (2002).

5. Ferguson expounds on empire at length in his *Empire* and in *Colossus*. See Chibber 2005 for a precise rebuttal of Ferguson's historical claims and historiographical methods. Ferguson's celebrity, based equally upon his egregious claims for the great benefits the British Empire enabled for their colonized populations and for his insistence that the US should be equally unembarrassed about claiming the "civilizational" burdens of empire, has proved productive for political thinkers across the globe, if only because they have been forced to rebut his historical arguments and his vision of the imperial future. For an Indian instance, see Chari 2008.

6. Adam Taylor has published a recent survey of the increasing US military footprint in Africa (Taylor 2014).

7. In an article in the Calcutta *Telegraph*, Ashok Mitra calls attention to the US refusal to close its base in Okinawa, in spite of the election pledge of the new Japanese Prime Minister, Yukio Hatoyama of the Democratic Party, who resigned in protest. In a comment on the US denial of Japan's sovereignty, Mitra writes:

> Getting rid of the American base in Okinawa has turned out to be a different story. . . . neither [Japan's] economic prowess nor its formal political sovereignty has been of any avail. . . . The US response to the notice served on them by the new Japanese administration to quit Okinawa . . . [was]: no, the United States will not oblige; Okinawa may be Japanese territory, Japan may be a fully independent and an economically powerful nation, the Americans could not care less; never mind the electoral verdict of the Japanese people, Okinawa will remain an American naval base, maybe for eternity, just like the one at Guantanamo in communist Cuba. (2010)

8. Raja Mohan derives his sense of "the 'India Center' concept in the British imperial defense" from Brobst. Brobst's book elaborates ideas about geopolitical security centered around the geographical landmass of India, as well as the sea lanes it might control, that were developed most fully by Sir Olaf Caroe, who was foreign secretary to Britain's government of India during World War II and then Britain's last governor of the North West Frontier Province. Caroe's thinking, forged by the priorities of Britain's empire, looked beyond its end to a time when, as "a counterpoise to Soviet and increasingly Chinese power consolidated in the Asian heartland, India would remain pivotal in the maintenance of a global balance between land and sea power" (xiv). Brobst argues that there is today afoot a "New Great Game for control of [Central Asia's] oil and gas," in which the "United States has assumed many of the attributes of Britain's former role in Asia, but the subcontinent remains the central strategic space" (2005: 147).

9. While historians of empire have recorded the adroit use of Indian soldiers by the East India Company and then by the British imperial administration to gain territories and extend their control within India, it is only recently that scholarly analysis has detailed the extensive deployment of Indian soldiers outside of the boundaries of British India and examined the consequences of such deployment for politics in India and in

Britain. As this scholarship makes clear, these forces were not simply a perk of empire, but crucial to its extension and maintenance, particularly during World War I and II. David Omissi points out that by the end of the First World War, over nine hundred thousand Indian troops were serving overseas and that they "fought and died in France and Flanders, in Mesopotamia and Palestine, at Gallipoli and Salonika, and in Egypt, the Sudan, and East Africa" (2007: 74). Daniel Marston points out that between "1939 and 1945, the [Indian] army expanded from two hundred thousand to more than 2.5 million men and officers," who destroyed the Imperial Japanese Army in Burma, fought against the Italians and Germans in North and East Africa and Italy, and took and held important oil fields in Iraq and Iran (2007: 102).

10. The election of Narendra Modi as prime minister of India has added impetus to US attempts to sell arms to India. Chuck Hagel, the US defense secretary, visited New Delhi in early August 2014 to cement military ties, and news reports were clear that this visit was part of efforts made by the US "to secure greater military cooperation with India as its seeks to counter growing Chinese firepower in Asia." See for instance the AFP report, "Hagel in India to Boost Defence Ties, Trade; Meets PM," published in the *Hindustan Times* on August 8, 2014 (http://www.hindustantimes.com/india-news/defence -deals-on-agenda-us-defence-secretary-hagel-meets-sushma/article1-1249580.aspx).

11. A highly readable, humane account of the brutal imperial adventures of even a tiny European principality—in this case the Belgium of King Leopold—is available in Hochschild (1999).

12. A signal instance is the 1953 CIA-backed coup d'état that deposed Mohammad Mosaddegh, the democratically elected prime minister of Iran, when he moved to nationalize the British-controlled Anglo-Iranian Oil Company (the precursor of British Petroleum, now branded BP).

13. For analysts of postcolonial history, two other military campaigns that moved to incorporate territories within the "landmass" of India, so to speak, are less controversial: the "police action" that annexed another princely state, Hyderabad, to India in September 1948, and the liberation of Goa from Portuguese colonialism in December 1961. Goans had in any case struggled for years against the dictatorial regime of António Salazar, and in Hyderabad, the Nizam's equally autocratic regime had alienated the majority of those he ruled, with sections of the peasantry, particularly in Telengana, already in revolt against landowners owing fealty to him. Once incorporated into India, there have been no secessionist movements in either territory, as opposed to the sustained attempts made by large sections of Kashmiris to determine their political future outside the status granted them by the Indian Constitution.

14. Punjab saw equivalent moments, as for instance in 1984 when, during Operation Bluestar (the attack on the Golden Temple in Amritsar to wrest it from Jarnail Singh Bhindranwale and his followers), all civilian administration, including police authority, was suspended. Even when the army was not deployed, the movement for an independent Khalistan was destroyed primarily by police and paramilitary power rather than via a political process.

15. China provides a contemporary comparison: the military has been used to suppress Tibetan and Uighur movements for self-determination. This mode of forced

"assimilation" complements China's global ambitions: as the history of modern imperial nations suggests, any nation that aspires to superpower status cannot countenance democratic self-assertion among minority populations within its borders.

16. Ireland wrested its independence from the British Empire in 1923 after a long and occasionally bloody struggle, with six counties in Northern Ireland still under British rule. More recently, there has been a tenuous devolution of power in Northern Ireland too, which has allowed for peace after many years of conflict between Irish Catholics and the pro-British Protestants. Since 1998 the Scots have had their own parliament in Edinburgh. In September 2014, 45 percent of voters voted for Scottish independence, though the majority voted to remain part of the United Kingdom. More surprisingly (given that they were conquered and colonized by Edward I in the late thirteenth century) the Welsh too have moved to recover their separate political identity; since 1999, a Welsh assembly with substantial budgetary and legislative powers now meets in Cardiff. In these ways, Great Britain has moved towards a more 'postcolonial' conception of the power relations between center and provinces than seems possible in India.

17. *Bloomberg Businessweek* reported on a pledge made by the Indian Home Secretary to enable $80 billion in investments in heavy industry by defeating, within three years, the Maoist rebels who defend the largely tribal and forested territories where minerals are to be mined and industries located (see Pradhan and Kumar 2010).

18. For an account of the new "commodity frontier," see Padel and Das 2010.

19. B. K. Nehru, once governor of J & K, has this to say in his autobiography: "From 1953 to 1975, Chief Ministers of that State had been nominees of Delhi. Their appointment to that post was legitimized by the holding of farcical and totally rigged elections in which the Congress Party led by Delhi's nominee was elected by huge majorities" (Nehru 1997: 614–15).

Sanjay Kak (2010), a noted documentary filmmaker and Kashmir-watcher, writes:
> In the first election of 1952, under the dominating presence of Sheikh Abdullah, his National Conference was a political party that had willingly stepped in as a lynchpin of India's strategy to "retain" Kashmir, and the party won every single seat in that first election. "Won" is too facile a description of what happened, because only two out of the seventy-five seats were actually contested. The rest had a walk-over. (The opposition, such as it was, was simply not allowed to file their nominations.) This happened with the active concurrence of the Government in New Delhi, because in these early days of India's freedom, with the world looking over his shoulder, Prime Minister Jawaharlal Nehru desperately needed to demonstrate the legitimacy of India's control over Kashmir. Sheikh Abdullah, at that time a personal friend of Nehru, took over as the Prime Minister of Jammu & Kashmir. . . .
>
> When the next election came by in 1957, Nehru may have had some second thoughts about what he had started off. He is said to have written to Bakshi Ghulam Mohammed suggesting that he generously lose a few seats, so that the image of the world's largest democracy was not tarnished. But such cosmetic

niceties cut little ice with the National Conference. It was unstoppable, and won sixty-eight seats. Half of these were uncontested.

In 1962 the National Conference repeated this strategy, and won seventy seats. Again half were uncontested.

A twisted template had been set, and democracy had become an early victim. Kak also reminds us that in the 1967 Assembly elections, held after G. M. Sadiq had merged the National Conference with the Congress in 1965, the Congress won sixty-one seats, of which fully fifty-three were uncontested. In the first four elections, "voter turnout . . . was consistently low, never more than 25 percent of the electorate."

20. This is not only a question of aggressive, even murderous, forms of policing, but also of an expansion of bases into large swathes of farm land and orchards that are now denied to their owners. Access routes to adjoining working areas are occasionally blocked by undefined security considerations, and the free movement of villagers impeded (see Navlakha 2007).

21. That Indian security officials have been liaising, and learning from, the equivalents in the Israeli Defence Force (IDF) is no longer news; however, it is still startling to hear an ex-official of the IDF Advocate General's Corps describe his surprise at the belligerent rules of engagement (vis-à-vis civilians suspected of links with militants) laid out for him by generals of the Indian army (see Nayar 2010).

22. Since 1972, an amendment gives the central government the right to declare an area "disturbed," even over the objections of the concerned state government, and thus to apply the act. For a useful history and assessment of the AFSPA, see the South Asia Human Rights Documentation Center report, "Armed Forces Special Powers Act."

23. For a disturbing reminder of the implications of the recent advocacy of the AFSPA by serving armed forces personnel, see Noorani 2010.

24. Mirani writes: "NHPC, sometimes referred to as the East India Company of Kashmir for the imperial manner in which it exploits resources in the region, is strongly disliked as most of its income comes from its Kashmir-based power projects, while Kashmir itself reels in darkness."

25. A great deal of central government funding actually goes into the maintenance of the security infrastructure at the borders, as well as the massive logistical apparatus required to service that infrastructure. For an argument that suggests that Jammu and Kashmir is able to use only 30 percent of these central grants on social spending because 70 percent is tied up in salaries, security expenditure, power, and interest payments, see Talib 2010.

Army soldiers leave the site of a gun battle | Audora Kulgam, February 2012

Zahid Mukhtar

Kus badlāvi sōn taqdīr

Vuni chu obras kālu' buth
Vuni chi zu'tsu' qādas andar

Vuni chi ru'khi pẙṭh śīnu' tshaṭh
Khūn akhtābas tsu'hān

Vuni chi rātsan manz gatsān
Mōtu'k ālav tsọpāri

Vuni chi rōyas zūni tim
Ākhratu' suri tāru'ku'ki

Vuni chu ṣubhuk nūr phoṭ
Rātu' krīlan tsōpmut

Vuni chu pōśan muśuk zan
Tāpu' tẙnglan manz buzān

Vuni vuṭhan pẙṭh ālvu'k
Harf chi tsharṭu'tsharṭh karān

Vuni chu bōnẙn śrād āz
Vuni chu śihlis tsūrimēy

Vuni Hōkarsar, Dal, Vọlạr
Rātshdar su'nzi śrāki tal

Vuni chi Dargāh, Khānyār
Bankarō ạndi ạndi vạlith

Vuni chu Sultān hīri pẙṭh
Kūṭ rath vālun chạlith

Vuni chu Hamdānas minār
Vunlital sōruy khu'ṭith

Zahid Mukhtar

Who Will Change Our Destiny?

Even now, the cloud has a dark face
Even now, the sun's rays are in prison

Even now, on the borders, snow-winds
are sucking blood from the sun

Even now—it happens in the nights—
Calls of death sound everywhere

Even now, the face of the moon
is scarred by bloodied stars

Even now, the light-basket[1] of the dawn
has been chewed by the night-bat

Even now, flowers seem to reek
roasted in the sun's cinders

Even now, upon lips
the letters of the call are restless

Even now—today—chinars have their *shrādh*
Even now, their shade is mourned on its *chŏrim*[2]

Even now, Hokarsar, Dal, Wular[3]
are under the watchman's blade

Even now, the Dargah,[4] Khanyar[5]
are wrapped end-to-end with bunkers

Even now, on the steps of the Sultan[6]
so much blood to be washed down

Even now, Hamdan's[7] minaret
is hidden entirely in the fog

Vuni chi khōtsān sạn śuri
Gotshnu' kānh vethi dẙun bạrith

Vuni chu prẙth kānh margzār
Lālu' zāran pẙṭh rivān

Vuni tsu' kath chukh hol gạnḍith
Bạ̄th Kạśmīru'ki gẙvān

Even now, our children are afraid
that someone might throw them in the Vyeth

Even now, every last graveyard
weeps over crimson gardens[8]

Even now, why do you so resolutely
sing songs of Kashmir?

....

Published in *Sheeraza* (Kashmiri) 40:1–3 (2007), 140–41. Also published in Zahid Mukhtar, *Tanbri Halm* (Srinagar, 2009).

Zahid Mukhtar was born in 1956 in Chini Chowk, Anantnag. He graduated from the Government Degree College in Anantnag in 1979 and worked for a while in the Public Health Engineering Department. He publishes short stories, essays, and poetry in both Kashmiri and Urdu. His most recent volume is *Tishnagi* (2014).

NOTES

1. Idiomatically, *nūr-phot* is used to suggest something that is right and good (as opposed to *shikas-phot*).

2. The *shrādh* is a Pandit ceremony to mourn their dead; the *chŏrim* (the fourth day after a death) is an important day in Muslim ceremonies of mourning.

3. The Hokarsar, Dal, and Wular are all lakes in Kashmir.

4. The Hazratbal shrine on the banks of the Dal lake.

5. The Dastgeer Sahib shrine in Khanyar, Srinagar.

6. The Makhdoom Sahib shrine on the Koh-e-Maran hill in Srinagar.

7. The Khanqah of Shah-i-Hamadan in Srinagar.

8. The Mughals planted tulips to fashion a *lal-zaar*, a red-garden; in Kashmiri, the term is also used idiomatically to refer to a dear one.

Som Nath Bhat "Veer"

nov subaḥ phọli

Kālu'pẏṭhu' cī kitsh vẏkhu'ts vānākh rāth
Rāṭs hund pot paḥar gaṭu' zạli

Thāvmu'ts ạs māntu'rāvith śīntsrāvith kāyināth
kāvrēmu'ts sarzamīn ḍajmu'ts hẏsav

Ghāb tārakh nab nu' kuni ākāśigang
Kālu' obran nāl volmut āvrith śanvay taraf

Ạchdaran hu'ndi ạs vaḥrith
Ḍōnṭhu' chapu' mạnzi rūdu' traṭu' gagrāyi grẏni

Kot gatshan bēcāru' bēgar rāh musāfir kot gatshan
Vānu' penjan pẏṭh voṭhān tim vūri vūri rāṭirātas

Natu' zacal khū'man andar
Kuli gọgar ālẏn andar śrepith karān zip' jānvār

Chus divān lari phirni kun zon jānvār
Kamli tal yath zạdi tu'vuli

Khū'mu' kūnjas manz me ditsmu'ts śāndu' sīr
Karsanā phọli gāś bulbul kar pican

Ḍōnṭhu' tsādar zantu' kani śāvay karān
Hōś kạritav yithu' nabā gari nēri kānh

Chusbu' prārān
Karsanā gatshi mandru'cē gaṇṭāyi ṭhas

Masjidi manz diyi bạngi bang
Bod chu day al-lāhu akbar gatshi kanan

Saḥru' waqtan siryi sakhrith
Cāri beyi lāqam rathas

Som Nath Bhat "Veer"

A New Day Will Dawn

Since last evening, what a devious, threatening night
The last, darkest hour of the night

We had kept consecrated and orderly the universe
Trembling the blessed land, its consciousness lost

Disappeared the starry sky, nowhere the Milky Way
Dark clouds have enveloped and busied all the six directions

The pythons' mouths are open
In hailstorms, though sheets of rain, in the thunderstorm

Where will the poor and unhoused wayfarers go, where will they go
From the thresholds of shops, they leave for faraway places all night

Or inside ragged tents
In tree-holes, shrinking, birds doze

I toss-and-turn, a lone bird
Once under the blanket, torn and holey

In a corner of the tent, my pillow a brick
When will the light dawn, when the bulbul sing

The hailstorm seems to rain stones
Beware, let no one leave the house

I am waiting
When will the temple bell sound

From the mosque, the muezzin will call
God is Great, Allah-o-Akbar, ears will hear

At dawn, the sun prepares
Pulls on the chariot's reins

Vuni nu' vuni sognẏār kari yiyi sāsu'gāś
Chalu'vadu'r gatshi kālu'obras trāvi dav

Volru' kẏn malran vuniundur gav sẏṭhāh
Voni bihan loti pāṭhi dẏv rasu' pursakūn

Voni pholu'ni hẏn mālu' nānpan bālu' tēg
Vuzmalu'ni joś gatshi Afarwat bālu' gāb

Bāmbrith beyi obru' longi chali chali gatshan
Nal nakh phuṭith phambu' tombi zabarvan bālu' pẏṭhi

Just about now, a soft light will spread
The dark clouds will be scattered, will flee

The waves of the Wular have slept badly long enough
Now they will settle quietly, calmly, peacefully

Now they will bloom, the hill tops will wear bright garlands
Lightning's edge will disappear in the Apharwat hills[1]

Scurrying again, banks of clouds will dissipate
Limbs broken, they will turn cotton puffs over the Zabarwan hills[2]

·················

Published in *Aalav* (Kashmiri) (Nov.-Dec. 2003), 40–41.

Som Nath Bhat "Veer" was born in 1940 in Lok Bhawan, Dooru, Anantnag. After receiving an MA in Hindi he worked as a teacher and retired as headmaster of the Government High School, Dooru. He also read radio news in Urdu and Kashmiri. He has published several volumes of poetry and prose including *Deewan-e-Veer* (collected works).

NOTES

1. The Gulmarg hills.
2. The Srinagar hills.

A procession of lit torches marks the annual festival of the Sufi saint Sakhi
Zain-uddin Wali | Aishmuqam, April 2013

Coda: A Time without Soldiers

"A Pastoral" is one of the poems of loss, longing, and imagined redemption in Agha Shahid Ali's brilliant volume on Kashmir, *The Country without a Post Office*. Shahid's poem registers the pain of a Kashmir racked by violence, but choses to look forward, to a time without soldiers, to a return of all those Hindus and Muslims who had been displaced in fear, to a reassertion of age-old friendships and ties of mutuality. He addressed it to me (as a friend and a Pandit) and it is, in the most profound sense, an invitation and a deferred promise:

> We shall meet again, in Srinagar,
> By the gates of the Villa of Peace,
> our hands blossoming into fists
> till the soldiers return the keys
> and disappear. Again we'll enter
> our last world, the first that vanished
>
> in our absence from the broken city.

I have thought often of the deeply ironic title of the poem: once, Kashmir could only be found in pastoral poetry and art, which dematerialized human lives and social contradictions into the rustling of brooks and the lapping edges of lakes, the green carpets of meadows, the orderly lines of flowers in well-laid gardens, the tall trees of the hills and the snows of the high mountains, and the unchanging timelessness of a land outside history.

In contrast, in Shahid's poem Srinagar is a city of blight and blood, and requires humane, therapeutic action: "We'll tear our shirts for tourniquets/ and bind the open thorns, warm the ivy/into roses." There is no flowering garden here, for the gardener now lives only as a voice who confirms rumors of the occasion of his death: "It's true, my death, at the mosque entrance,/in the massacre, when the Call to Prayer/opened the floodgates." This is a city of search posts and of cemeteries with "hurried graves/with no names." Even spring brings with it not renewal but a new and astonishing herald: "the mountain falcon" that rips open, "in mid-air, the blue magpie," and carries it limp from its talons.

Once home, what do we find but—and this is a recurrent theme in Shahid's poetry—lost letters. Or rather, letters that have been delivered in the absence of the addressee, for the mailman was sure "we'd return to answer them." When these not quite dead letters speak, they echo the "plaintive cry" uttered first by the bird:

See how your world has cracked.
Why aren't you here? Where are you? Come back.

Is history deaf there, across the oceans?

But now we are home, the poem says, our keys are opening locks, and we walk past dusty mirrors and light lamps, and view dimly "The glass map of our country." There are pictures on the staircases as we climb up, and they are of our ancestors, and they too speak:

Their wish
was we return—forever!—and inherit (Quick, the bird
will say) that to which we belong, not like this—
to get news of our death after the world's.

Not long after Shahid died in December 2001, I returned to Srinagar, and found the city he mourns so poignantly in "A Pastoral" and the other poems in *Country without a Post Office*. We dusted the rooms and pictures in our ancestral home, and were glad that those who gazed down at us had not lived to experience the ravages of the last two decades. They would not know or understand this Kashmir, with its murderous history and its terrible schisms between populations and families. What I saw then moved me to write about Kashmir, and I continue to do so, if only to understand for myself all that turned Kashmir, and Srinagar, into the armed camp it continues to be. And I think Shahid's invitation knew, well before the fact, that such a moment must come, which is why "A Pastoral" is also a promise of a future of rediscovery and renewal, a future without soldiers, a future of shared hopes and lives.

And Shahid, who is no more, does he keep his promise to return, to renew, to heal? Quite simply, he does, for no one knows better than a poet the power of words, of the speaking voice, of poetry as the pulse of life beyond death. I hear his voice still, and I know, as the years pass, Kashmiris (and not only Kashmiris) hear in his poems their passion, their loss, their anger, their determination, and their aspiration. In their varied voices, as they read and celebrate Shahid, I hear the future to which he, so beloved of many, bore powerful witness. And it is toward that future that I, and others like me, write when as we think about the past, the present, and the future in Kashmir.

A woman walks past a mustard field as paramilitary soldier stands guard |
Anantnag, April 2013

Bibliography

Ahmed, Mudasir. "Massive Crackdown in Kashmir to Guarantee 'Peaceful' Modi Visit." *The Wire*. November 6, 2015. Accessed on November 6, 2015. http://thewire.in/2015/11/06/massive-crackdown-in-kashmir-to-guarantee-peaceful -modi-visit-14890/

Ahmed, Sara (2004). "Affective Economies." *Social Text* 22:2, 117–139.

Ali, Agha Shahid (1997). *The Country without a Post Office*. New York: Norton.

Ali, Agha Shahid (2000). *Ravishing Disunities: Real Ghazals in English*. Hanover: Wesleyan University Press.

Ali, Agha Shahid (2009). *The Veiled Suite: The Collected Poems*. New Delhi: Penguin.

Amin, Syed and A. W. Khan (2009). "Life in Conflict Characteristics of Depression in Kashmir." *International Journal of Health Sciences* 3:2, 213–23. Accessed on June 10, 2014. http://www.ncbi.nlm.nih.gov/pmc/articles/PMC3068807/.

"Armed Forces Special Powers Act: A Study in National Security Tyranny." South Asia Human Rights Documentation Center. Accessed on August 10, 2010. htm://www.hrdc.net/sahrdc/resources/armed__forces.htm.

Aziz, Afaq (2003). Ed. *Naghma te Beath* (*Musical Songs*). Srinagar: Writers Organization for Research and Development.

"Begin Healing Process in J&K, Says U.N. Special Rapporteur." *The Hindu*. January 22, 2011. Accessed January 24, 2011. http://www.thehindu.com/news /national/article1109388.ece.

Bhat, M. Ashraf (2014). "Memories of Kashmir: Past, Present and Hope." *Countercurrents*. Accessed on March 31, 2014. http://www.countercurrents.org /bhat070314.htm.

Brass, Paul R (2003). "The Partition of India and Retributive Genocide in the Punjab, 1946–47: Means, Methods, and Purposes." *Journal of Genocide Research* 5:1, 71–101.

Brobst, Peter John (2005). *The Future of the Great Game: Sir Olaf Caroe, India's Independence and the Defense of Asia*. Akron, Ohio: University of Akron Press.

Bukhari, Parvaiz (2010). "Kashmir 2010, the Year of Killing Youth." *The Nation*. September 22, 2010. Accessed on January 25, 2011. http://www.thenation.com /article/154964/kashmir-2010-year-killing-youth.

Canny, Nicholas (1988). *Kingdom and Colony: Ireland in the Atlantic World 1560–1800*. Baltimore: Johns Hopkins University Press.

Canny, Nicholas (2001). *Making Ireland British 1580–1650*, Oxford: Oxford University Press.

Caruth, Cathy (1995). Ed. *Trauma: Explorations in Memory*. Baltimore: Johns Hopkins University Press.

Caruth, Cathy (1996). *Unclaimed Experience: Trauma, Narrative, and History*. Baltimore: Johns Hopkins University Press.

Chari, Chandra (2008). Ed. *War, Peace and Hegemony in a Globalized World: The Changing Balance of Power in the Twenty-First Century*. Abingdon: Routledge.

Chattha, Ilyas (nd). "Terrible Fate: 'Ethnic Cleansing' of Jammu Muslims in 1947." *Journal of Pakistan Vision* 10 (1): 117–40. Accessed on January 28, 2011. http://pu.edu.pk:82/punjab/home/journal/12/Previous-Issue.html.

Chattha, Ilyas (2011). *Partition and Locality: Violence, Migration, and Development in Gujranwala and Sialkot 1947–1961*. Karachi: Oxford University Press.

Chaudhary, Amit Anand Choudhary (2015). "Only 1 Pandit Family Returned to Valley in 25 Years." *Times of India*. November 1, 2015. Accessed on November 2, 2015.

Chibber, Vivek (2005). "The Good Empire: Should We Pick Up Where the British Left Off?" *Boston Review*, February/March, 30–34.

Cleary, Joe (2002). *Literature, Partition, and the Nation State: Culture and Conflict in Ireland, Israel, and Palestine*. Cambridge: Cambridge University Press.

Copland, Ian (1998). "The Further Shores of Partition: Ethnic Cleansing in Rajasthan, 1947." *Past and Present* 160:1, 203–239.

Corruccini, Robert S. and Samvit S. Kaul (1990). *Halla: Demographic Consequences of the Partition of the Punjab, 1947*. Lanham; University Press of America.

Davoine, Françoise and Jean-Max Gaudillière (2004). *History Beyond Trauma*. Trans. Susan Fairfield. New York: Other Press.

de Jong, Kaz, Saskia van de Kam, Nathan Ford, Kamalini Lokuge, Silke Fromm, Renate van Galen, Brigg Reilley and Rolf Kleber (2008). "Conflict in the Indian Kashmir Valley II: Psychosocial Impact." *Conflict and Health* 2:11. Accessed on May 23, 2014. http://www.conflictandhealth.com/content/2/1/11.

"Demand for Changes in AFSPA for Political Gains: Army Chief." *The Daily News and Analysis*, Mumbai. 26 June 2010. Accessed on August 10, 2010. http://www.dnaindia.com/india/report_afspa-withdrawal-demand-is-for-political-gains-army-chief_1401439.

Fassin, Didier and Richard Rechtman (2009). *The Empire of Trauma: An Inquiry into the Condition of Victimhood*. Trans. Rachel Gomme. Princeton: Princeton University Press.

Ferguson, Niall (2003a): "The Empire Slinks Back." *New York Times Magazine* 27. April 2003. Accessed on July 7, 2010. http://www.nytimes.com/2003/04/27/magazine/27EMPIRE.html?pagewanted=1?pagewanted=1.

Ferguson, Niall (2003b). *Empire: The Rise and Demise of the British World Order and the Lessons for Global Power*. New York: Basic Books.

Ferguson, Niall (2004). *Colossus: The Rise and Fall of the American Empire*. New York: Penguin.

Gangahar, Manisha (2013). "Decoding Violence in Kashmir." *Economic and Political Weekly* 48:4, 35–42.

Ganguly, Sumit (1996). "Explaining the Kashmir Insurgency: Political Mobilization and Institutional Decay." *International Security* 21:2, 76–107.

Gigoo, Siddhartha (2011). *The Garden of Solitude*. Delhi: Rupa & Co.

Gigoo, Siddhartha and Varad Sharma (2015). Eds. *A Long Dream of Home: The Persecution, Exodus and Exile of Kashmiri Pandits*. New Delhi: Bloomsbury Books.

Guardian (UK). "US Embassy Cables: US Argues against Visa for Kashmiri 'Paramilitary'." Accessed on January 24, 2011. http://www.guardian.co.uk/world/us-embassy-cables-documents/110718.

Harding, Thomas (2008). "Chinese Nuclear Submarine Base." *The Telegraph*. May 1, 2008. Accessed on June 18, 2010. http://www.telegraph.co.uk/news/world-news/asia/china/1917167/Chinese-nuclear-submarine-base.html.

Hasan, Khalid (2005). "Jammu 1947: Gone But Not Forgotten." Accessed on January 20, 2011. http://www.khalidhasan.net/2005/05/27/jammu-1947-gone-but-not-forgotten/.

Hassan, Manzoor-ul- (2013). "Kashmir Has One Lakh Conflict Trauma Patients." *Rising Kashmir*. September 14, 2013. Accessed on September 15, 2013. http://www.risingkashmir.in/kashmir-has-one-lakh-conflict-trauma-patients/.

Hazarika, Sanjay (1994). *Strangers of the Mist: Tales of War and Peace from India's North-east*. New Delhi: Penguin Books.

Hechter, Daniel (1999). *Internal Colonialism: The Celtic Fringe in British National Development*, 2nd ed. New Brunswick, N.J.: Transaction Publishers.

Hochschild, Adam (1999). *King Leopold's Ghost: A Story of Greed, Terror, and Heroism in Colonial Africa*. New York: Mariner Books.

Hoskote, Ranjit (2011). Trans. and Ed. *I, Lalla: The Poems of Lal Děd*. New Delhi: Penguin Books.

Human Rights Watch (2006). *"Everyone Lives in Fear": Patterns of Impunity in Jammu and Kashmir*. September 12, 2006. Accessed on May 24, 2014. http://www.hrw.org/reports/2006/09/11/everyone-lives-fear-0.

Human Rights Watch (1996), *India's Secret Army in Kashmir: New Patterns of Abuse Emerge in the Conflict*. May 1, 1996. Accessed on January 24, 2011. http://www.unhcr.org/refworld/docid/3ae6a8558.html.

Hussain, Aijaz (2015). "1 Dead in Kashmir Protest as India's Leader Promises Aid." *AP News*. November 7, 2015. Accessed on November 7, 2015. http://bigstory.ap.org/article/a579f72b11f34bdc9773cf4b41923ec9/indian-kashmir-high-alert-prime-minister-modis-visit

Huttenback, Robert A (2004). *Kashmir and the British Raj 1847–1947*. Karachi: Oxford University Press.

International People's Tribunal on Human Rights and Justice in Indian-Administered Kashmir and The Association of Parents of Disappeared Persons. *Structures Of*

Violence: The Indian State in Jammu and Kashmir. September 2015. Accessed on November 15, 2015. http://www.jkccs.net/structures-of-violence-the-indian-state -in-jammu-and-kashmir-2/

International People's Tribunal on Human Rights and Justice in Kashmir. *Buried Evidence: Unknown, Unmarked, and Mass Graves in Indian-Administered Kashmir.* December 2, 2009. Accessed on January 24, 2011. http://www .kashmirprocess.org/reports/graves/01Front.html.

International Tribunal for Human Rights and Justice in Indian-Administered Kashmir and the Association of Parents of Disappeared Persons. *Alleged Perpetrators: Stories of Impunity in Jammu and Kashmir.* December 6, 2012. Accessed on May 24, 2014. http://kashmirprocess.org/reports/alleged _Perpetrators.pdf.

Jaleel, Muzamil (2002). "Poetry in Commotion." July 29, 2002. Accessed on April 3, 2014. http://www.theguardian.com/world/2002/jul/29/kashmir.india.

Jamal, Arif (2009). *Shadow War: The Untold Story of Jihad in Kashmir.* New York: Melville House.

Jean-Klein, Iris (2001). "Nationalism and Resistance: The Two Faces of Everyday Activism in Palestine during the Intifada." *Cultural Anthropology* 16:1, 83–126.

Jha, Prem Shankar (1998). *Kashmir 1947: Rival Versions of History.* New Delhi: Oxford University Press.

Joseph, Manu (2012). "Sorry, Kashmir Is Happy." April 21, 2012. *Open Magazine.* Accessed on August 13, 2013. http://www.openthemagazine.com/article/nation /sorry-kashmir-is-happy.

Kak, Sanjay (2014). "Ballot Bullet Stone: What Will the Coming Elections Mean for Kashmir?" *The Caravan Magazine.* September 1, 2014. Accessed on November 1, 2014. http://www.caravanmagazine.in/reportage/ballot-bullet-stone.

Kak, Sanjay (2011). Ed. *Until My Freedom Has Come: The New Intifada in Kashmir.* New Delhi: Penguin.

Kak, Sanjay (2010). Personal communication. August 5, 2010.

Kaul, Jayalal (1973). *Lal Děd.* New Delhi: Sahitya Akademi.

Kaul, Suvir (2010). "Days in Srinagar." *Outlook.* August 6, 2010. Accessed on January 24, 2011. http://www.outlookindia.com/article.aspx?266544.

Kaul, Suvir (2011). "Indian Empire (and the Case of Kashmir)." *Economic and Political Weekly* 47:13, 66–75.

Kaul, Suvir (2013). "To Walk Past the Threatening Gaze." *Outlook.* August 5, 2013. Accessed on January 18, 2014. http://www.outlookindia.com/article.aspx ?287103.

Khan, Akbar (1970). *Raiders in Kashmir.* Islamabad: National Book Foundation.

Khan, Yasmin (2007). *The Great Partition: The Making of India and Pakistan.* New Haven: Yale University Press.

"Khandaypora family still claims slain LeT commander." *Kashmir Reader.* October 31, 2015. Accessed on October 31, 2015. http://www.kashmirreader.com/News /SingleNews?NewsID=336&callto=Top

Kirmayer, Lawrence J (1996). "Landscapes of Memory: Trauma, Narrative, and Dissociation." In *Tense Past: Cultural Essays in Trauma and Memory*. Eds. Paul Antze and Michael Lambek. New York: Routledge, 173–199.

Kleinman, Arthur, Veena Das, and Margaret Lock (1998). *Social Suffering*. Delhi: Oxford University Press.

LaCapra, Dominick (2001). *Writing History, Writing Trauma*. Baltimore: Johns Hopkins University Press.

Lamb, Alastair (1966). *Crisis in Kashmir 1947 to 1966*. London: Routledge and Kegan Paul.

Lateef, Adil (2013). "From Stones to Guns, a 'Martyr' at Home." *The Kashmir Walla*. April 19, 2013. Accessed on Oct. 31, 2013. http://www.thekashmirwalla.com/2013/04/from-stones-to-guns-a-martyr-at-home/.

Marston, Daniel P (2007). "A Force Transformed: The Indian Army and the Second World War." In Marston and Sundaram, 102–122.

Marston, Daniel P., and Chandar S. Sundaram (2007). Eds. *A Military History of India and South Asia*. Bloomington: Indiana University Press.

Mathur, Shubh (2014). Ed. *Memory and Hope: New Perspectives on the Kashmir Conflict. Race and Class* 56.

Mayaram, Shail (1997). *Resisting Regimes: Myth, Memory, and the Shaping of a Muslim Identity*. New York: Oxford University Press.

Mirani, Haroon (2009). "Race to the Death over Kashmir Waters." *Asia Times Online*. January 13, 2009. Accessed on August 12, 2010. (http://www.atimes.com/atimes/South_Asia/KA13Df01.html).

Misri, Deepti (2014). " 'This Is Not a Performance!' Public Mourning and Visual Spectacle in Kashmir." In *Beyond Partition: Gender, Violence, and Representation in Postcolonial India*. Urbana: University of Illinois Press, 133–160.

Mitra, Ashok (2010): "Eye on the Main Chance." *The Telegraph*. June 21, 2010. Accessed on 21 June 2010. http://www.telegraphindia.com/1100621/jsp/opinion/story_12567735.jsp.

Mohan, C. Raja (2010). "The Return of the Raj." *The American Interest Online*. May–June 2010. Accessed on June 15, 2010. http://www.the-american-interest.com/article.cfm?piece=803.

Nabi, Peer Ghulam and Jingzhong Ye (2015). "Of Militarization, Counter-insurgency, and Land Grabs in Kashmir." *Economic and Political Weekly* 50:46–47, 58–64.

Narayan, Subhash and Rajeev Jayaswal (2010). "Border Tensions Hit ONGC's Exploration Work in J&K." *The Economic Times*. January 5, 2010. Accessed on September 21, 2010. http://economictimes.indiatimes.com/news/news-by-industry/energy/oil-gas/Border-tensions-hit-ONGCs-exploration-work-in-JK/articleshow/5411604.cms.

Navlakha, Gautam (2007). "State of Jammu and Kashmir's Economy." *Economic and Political Weekly* 42:40, 4034–4038.

Nayar, K. P. (2010). "Israeli Colonel Spills Kashmir Beans—Barak Policy-Maker Quotes Indian Officers on Use of Force in the Valley to Counter Terrorism."

Telegraph India. Accessed on September 16, 2010. http://www.telegraphindia
.com/1100806/jsp/nation/story_12777847.jsp.

NDTV Correspondent (2010). "Army Defends Armed Forces Special Powers Act."
NDTV. June 14, 2010. Accessed on August 9, 2010. http://www.ndtv.com/news
/india/army-defends-special-powers-act-31642.php.

Nehru, B. K. (1997). *Nice Guys Finish Second.* Delhi: Penguin.

Nickelsberg, Robert (2008). "PTSD in Kashmir." *Getty Images.* Accessed on May 28,
2014. http://www.reportagebygettyimages.com/features/ptsd-in-kashmir/.

Noorani, A. G. (2010). "Talkative Generals." *Frontline Magazine.* July 31–August 13,
2010. Accessed on September 13, 2010. http://www.hinduonnet.com/fline/fl2716
/stories/20100813271608200.htm.

Omissi, David (2007). "The Indian Army in the First World War, 1914–1918." In
Marston and Sundaram 74–87.

Padel, Felix and Das, Samarendra (2010). *Out of This Earth: East India Adivasis and
the Aluminium Cartel.* New Delhi: Orient Blackswan.

Pande, Ira (2011). Ed. *A Tangled Web: Jammu & Kashmir.* Delhi: HarperCollins.

Pandey, Gyanendra (2001). *Remembering Partition: Violence, Nationalism, and History in India.* Cambridge: Cambridge University Press.

Pandita, Rahul (2013). *Our Moon Has Blood Clots.* New Delhi: Random House.

Parrey, Arif Ayaz (2011). "A Victorious Campaign." In *Until My Freedom Has Come.*
Ed. Kak, 179–85.

Peer, Basharat (2009). *Curfewed Night.* Delhi: Random House.

Pradhan, Bibhudatta and Kumar, Santosh (2010). "Pillai to End Maoist Grip on
$80 Billion Investments." *Bloomberg Businessweek.* September 17, 2010. Accessed
on September 20, 2010. http://www.businessweek.com/news/2010-09-17/pillai
-to-end-maoist-grip-on-80-billion-investments.html.

"Rahman of Multan or Hajam of Kulgam, Qasim was 'true soldier of freedom
struggle': Bar." *Kashmir Reader.* October 31, 2015. Accessed on October 31,
2015. http://www.kashmirreader.com/News/SingleNews?NewsID=828
&callto=Area

Rai, Mridu (2004). *Hindu Rulers, Muslim Subjects: Islam, Rights, and the History of
Kashmir.* Princeton: Princeton University Press.

Raina, Badri (2014). "Secularism in the Valley." *Kashmir Times.* May 2, 2014. Accessed
on May 19, 2014. http://www.kashmirtimes.in/newsdet.aspx?q=31790.

"Riots Changed J&K Politics." Ved Bhasin interviewed by Shahnawaz Khan. *Kashmir Life.* October 3, 2009. Accessed on January 25, 2011. http://www.kashmirlife
.net/index.php?option=com_content&view=article&id=914%3Ariots-changed
-jak-politics&Itemid=163.

Robinson, Cabeiri (2013). *Body of Victim, Body of Warrior: Refugee Families and the
Making of Kashmiri Jihadists.* Berkeley: University of California Press.

Rothberg, Michael (2003). "'There Is No Poetry in This': Writing, Trauma, and
Home." In *Trauma at Home: After 9/11.* Ed. Judith Greenberg. Lincoln: University of Nebraska Press.

Sajad, Malik (2015). *Munnu: A Boy from Kashmir.* London: Fourth Estate.

Sandars, Christopher T (2000). *America's Overseas Garrisons: The Leasehold Empire.* Oxford: Oxford University Press.

Saraf, Muhammad Yusuf (2004). "The Jammu Massacres." In *Memory Lane to Jammu.* Eds. Rehmatullah Rad and Khalid Hasan. Lahore: Sang-e-Meel Publications, 161–97.

Schofield, Victoria (2010). *Kashmir in Conflict: India, Pakistan, and the Unending War.* London: I. B. Tauris.

Shah, Fahad, (2013). Ed. *Of Occupation and Resistance: Writing on Kashmir.* New Delhi: Westland and Tranquebar Press.

Snedden, Christopher (2001). "What Happened to Muslims in Jammu? Local Identity, 'the "Massacre" of 1947' and the Roots of the 'Kashmir Problem.'" *South Asia: Journal of South Asian Studies* 24:2, 111–134.

Snedden, Christopher (2013). *Kashmir: The Unwritten History.* New Delhi: HarperCollins Publishers.

Sonpar, Shobhna (2007). *Violent Activism: A Psychosocial Study of Ex-Militants in Jammu and Kashmir.* Report prepared in April for the Aman Public Charitable Trust (New Delhi).

Sridhar, Subrahmanyam (2005). "The Indus Water Treaty." *Security Research Review* 13. Accessed on August 28, 2010. http://www.bharat-rakshak.com/SRR/Volume13/sridhar.html.

Stephens, Ian (1953). *Horned Moon: An Account of a Journey through Pakistan, Kashmir, and Afghanistan.* London: Chatto and Windus.

Suri, Vivek (2009). "Geo-Scientists Recommend Resuming of Oil, Hydrocarbons Exploration in Kashmir." *Ground Report.* May 21, 2009. Accessed on September 22, 2010. http://www.groundreport.com/Media_and_Tech/Geo-scientists -recommend-resuming-of-oil-hydrocarb/2899592.

Symonds, Richard (2001). *In the Margins of Independence: A Relief Worker in India and Pakistan (1942–1949).* Karachi: Oxford University Press.

Talib, Arjimand Hussain (2010). "J&K's 'Dependency Syndrome' and the Unknown Facts." *Greater Kashmir.* July 21, 2010. Accessed on September 21, 2010. http://www.greaterkashmir.com/news/2010/Jul/21/j-k-s-dependency-syndrome -and-the-unknown-facts-25.asp.

Taylor, Adam (2014). "MAP; The U.S. Military Currently Has Troops in These African Countries." *Washington Post.* May 21, 2014. Accessed on May 26, 2014. http://www.washingtonpost.com/blogs/worldviews/wp/2014/05/21/map-the-u -s-currently-has-troops-in-these-african-countries/.

Tremblay, Reeta Chowdhari (2009). "Kashmir's Secessionist Movement Resurfaces: Ethnic Identity, Community Competition, and the State." *Asian Survey* 49:6, 924–950.

"Uranium Deposits Found in Ladakh, DAE Cautious." *Rediff India Abroad.* News report dated August 28, 2007. Accessed on August 30, 2010. http://www.rediff .com/news/2007/aug/28uranium.htm.

"U.S. Military Bases and Empire" (2002). *Monthly Review*. March 2002. Accessed on June 19, 2010. http://www.monthlyreview.org/0302editr.htm. See also Sandars 2000.

Varadarajan, Siddharth (2011). "The Fabric of Belonging." *The Hindu*. January 23, 2011. Accessed on January 24, 2011. http://www.hindu.com/2011/01/24/stories /2011012461840700.htm.

Varma, Saiba (2012). "Where There Are only Doctors: Counselors as Psychiatrists in Indian-Administered Kashmir." *Ethos* 40:4, 517–535.

Varma, Saiba (2013). "Springtime in Kashmir: A Tale of Two Protests." *Somatosphere*. June 3, 2013. Accessed on January 16, 2014. http://somatosphere.net/2013 /06/springtime-in-kashmir-a-tale-of-two-protests.html.

Waheed, Mirza (2011). *The Collaborator*. London: Viking.

Waheed, Mirza (2014). *The Book of Gold Leaves*. London: Viking.

Wani, Riyaz (2013). "In the Valley, after the Trauma, the Cost: Loss of Sex Drive." *Tehelka* 44:10. November 2. Accessed on January 9, 2014. http://www.tehelka .com/in-the-valley-after-the-trauma-the-cost-loss-of-sex-drive-2/.

Wax, Emily (2008). "In Kashmir, Conflict's Psychological Legacy: Mental Health Cases Swell in Two Decades." *The Washington Post*. September 1, 2008. Accessed on January 24, 2011. http://www.washingtonpost.com/wp-dyn/content/article /2008/08/31/AR2008083102088.html.

"Where should Abu Qasim lie buried? Villagers clash in Kashmir." *Hindustan Times*. October. 31, 2015. Accessed October 31, 2015. http://www.hindustantimes .com/punjab/where-should-abu-qasim-lie-buried-villagers-clash-in-kashmir /story-67W9TbiFYmHKoGYSCEyw8N.html

Zamindar, Vazira Fazila-Yacoobali (2007). *The Long Partition and the Making of Modern South Asia: Refugees, Boundaries, Histories*. New York: Columbia University Press.

Zutshi, Chitralekha (2004). *Languages of Belonging: Islam, Regional Identity, and the Making of Kashmir*. New York: Oxford University Press, 2004.

Zutshi, Chitralekha (2014). *Kashmir's Contested Pasts: Narratives, Sacred Geographies, and the Historical Imagination*. Delhi: Oxford University Press.

Index